When a Jew seeks wisdom:

The Sayings of the Fathers

ILLUSTRATIONS BY ERIKA WEIHS

When a Jew seeks wisdom:
The Sayings of the Fathers

by **SEYMOUR ROSSEL**

with Hyman Chanover and Chaim Stern

THE JEWISH VALUES SERIES

BEHRMAN HOUSE, INC. PUBLISHERS NEW YORK, N.Y.

Dedicated to
My mother and grandmother,
And to Willy, my father,
 who teach the path of the
 good heart by walking it.

Acknowledgments

The publishers wish to acknowledge Frances Long, whose astute judgment and constant effort helped create The Jewish Values Series.

Special thanks are due to Rabbi Martin A. Cohen of Hebrew Union College-Jewish Institute of Religion for his critical reading of the historical background material contained in "The Rabbis of Pirke Avot."

©Copyright 1975, by Behrman House, Inc.

Published by Behrman House, Inc.
1261 Broadway, New York, N.Y.
10 9 8 7 6 5 4   83 82 81 80 79 78 77
Manufactured in the United States of America

Library of Congress Cataloging in Publication Data
Rossel, Seymour.
  When a Jew seeks wisdom.

  (The Jewish values series)
  SUMMARY: An examination of Jewish tradition and values, using as a basis *Pirke Avot*, the teachings of rabbis who lived from 300 B.C.E. to 200 C.E.
  1. Jewish religious education—Text-books for adolescents. 2. Ethics, Jewish—Juvenile literature.
[1. Jewish religious education. 2. Ethics, Jewish]
I. Chanover, Hyman, joint author. II. Stern, Chaim, joint author. III. Title.
BM105.R64   296'.07   75-14119
ISBN 0-87441-089-4

Contents

If not now, when?

1   *What we value*   *9*

2   *Our freedom to choose*   *20*

3   *The struggle within us*   *27*

4   *Our tradition and* Pirke Avot   *34*

If I am not for myself,
who will be for me?

5   *The value of life*   *43*

6   *The value of awareness*   *55*

7   *The value of knowledge*   *64*

8   *The value of study*   *76*

9   *The value of courage*   *86*

10   *The value of patience*   *98*

11   *The value of love*   *111*

If I am only for myself,
what am I?

12   *The value of community*   *123*

13   *The value of possessions*   *134*

14 *The value of government*   144

15 *The value of judging*   159

16 *The value of delight*   171

17 *The value of sensitivity*   182

18 *The value of argument*   193

19 *The value of Torah*   203

20 *The value of peace*   211

21 *The value of labor*   219

If not now, when?

22 *Seeking the right course*   229

23 *Choosing life*   237

THE RABBIS OF PIRKE AVOT   247
A GLOSSARY OF SOURCES   251
INDEX   253

THE JEWISH VALUES SERIES

When a Jew seeks wisdom:
The Sayings of the Fathers

For two-and-a-half years the schools of Shammai and Hillel debated.
Should man have been created?

The school of Shammai said: It were better for man not to have been
created.

The school of Hillel said: It is better that man has been created.
They discussed and finally concluded:
It were better for man not to have been created,
but now that he is here, let him search his ways. [Erub. 13b]

And what does it mean, "Let him search his ways"?
A person must ask:

If I am not for myself, who will be for me?
And if I am only for myself, what am I?
And if not now, when? [Avot 1:14]

1

What we value

You are always changing. What is you cannot be fixed or frozen in any real way. While you are reading this sentence, your body is forming new cells, your hair and nails are growing, and chemical changes are taking place inside your body. Electrical impulses within your brain are translating these written words into thoughts and ideas. Your thoughts and ideas will change, too, as they come into contact with new information and new concepts. The things you care about will change.

How we may be shaped

We are shaped by ideas and thoughts. They flow swiftly around and through us like broad rivers. And as we shape and change these thought rivers into streams, rivulets, and ponds, they shape and change us, too. They cleave us into buttes and steppes, leaving us separated from our neighbors by grand canyons and arroyos.

We are complex

Human beings are worlds within worlds within worlds. Like trees, we put down roots and seek strength from the

MAN IN THE WORLD

We have a special place in the world. And we are aware of it! We share the earthly life of plants and animals, but our thoughts soar above them. Each man and woman, each boy and girl, is unique. Each reaches for a star in a special way.

soil of common ground in order to bear fruit in our season. Like animals, we learn to protect ourselves by taking on the color of our surroundings. Like insects, we busy ourselves in the work of our colony.

But unlike animals, we study the world around us, the universe in which we live, the mysteries we confront. We explore the earth for its treasures of knowledge—the remains of ancient civilizations, the relics of primitive mankind, the layers of petrified forest and fossilized sea life, and the subterranean outlines of prehistoric continents.

We study the skies, probing the depths of the universal void for intelligence and existence. We study ourselves, searching for a better understanding of disease and health, so that we might be healed and live, or seeking patterns of thought and behavior so that we might better understand one another. Those of us who search what is visible we call natural scientists.

Another search Some of us look into what is beyond seeing or feeling with the physical senses. We look into what we believe, into the things we seem to know without being able to prove them, into the things we value most. We seek answers for the presence of order and logic in the workings of the universe. We probe the meaning of the existence of the world and all that is in it. We study experience for a deeper truth—we seek the hidden within the simple, the extraordinary within the everyday, the sacred within the ordinary. Our eyes are trained to the sight of good and evil; and our minds question what good means and why evil exists. Those of us who search with this inner light are researchers, too, moral researchers.

Our survival as human beings depends on the success of both kinds of seeking—or even better, on a working relationship between the two. The history of many organized religions shows that values of the spirit must be more than mere beliefs, that they must be converted into behavior that reflects ordinary human goodness. Otherwise, overzealous religionists and mistaken "scientists of the spirit" can pervert religion so that it results in destruction, hurt, and waste. Only think of the terrible consequences of religious hostility and wars—the Crusades, the Inquisition, even the destruction of the tribe of Amalek in biblical times.

Seeking human survival

But depending on the natural scientists alone has also proved destructive. Even pure science has been turned to the building of machines of war and the invasion of the individual's personal life. Consider the atomic bomb, the missile and the jet fighter, the hand gun and the rifle. Or think of the wiretap and similar undercover eavesdropping devices.

To see how easily natural science may be perverted, we have considered the "scientists" of the Nazi Third Reich who used Jews and other minority group members in the concentration camps as human guinea pigs in their "scientific" experiments.

Scientists of the spirit and natural scientists can and should work together for the good of mankind. But they can only

Our actions speak

do so if the approach of each is pure. Then we can balance these two elements—natural and spiritual—within us. Our growing and changing will really be searching and learning. And the result of our searching will be action.

Actions tell us much about a person. Actions are a means of expression, a way of speaking. They tell us what a person treasures, what a person truly seeks, how a person feels, and what a person believes.

Patterns of action We choose some actions freely; others require difficult decisions. Some are a part of a way of life that we like. Others we learn by facing new problems—problems that cause fear or anxiety, amusement or amazement, want or desire, uncertainty or embarrassment.

Whether or not we realize it, most of our everyday actions fit a pattern. This pattern is designed by the group to teach us the values that the group holds to be important. We call the pattern by several names: custom, ritual, ceremony, law, values, and manners.

How the pattern works To see how this pattern works, think about how you greet people. When you meet someone for the first time, are introduced to a stranger by a friend, are congratulating an acquaintance, are welcoming a relative home from a journey, or bringing a new friend into your home, you usually greet that person with a smile. In our society, this is known to be a friendly action. It is common to us—and usually common to the person we are greeting.

Suppose that a friend came by and that, instead of smiling, you frowned or turned away. You would have given an impression. But it would not be one of friendliness. In our society, your friend might very well feel insulted.

Our manners and customs make it possible for us to live

in our society. In other societies, other customs are followed—and some of these would be strange to us.

In some Asian societies, the idea of "lending an ear" is turned into real action. The polite Asian listener tilts his head slightly, stretches out his neck, and turns an ear halfway toward the person who is speaking.

In some parts of Northern Germany this custom would be considered vulgar and insulting. Here the custom is for the person listening to face the speaker directly; to keep both eyes staring straight at the speaker's face; and to sit with the spine upright, as if at attention.

To see just how different this is from our pattern, try using these "manners" on one of your friends at the next opportunity. What we think of as "good" manners are almost always the ones that are familiar to us: the ones we have been taught by our parents and by our loved ones, by our society and by our friends. Other people's manners seem strange, and perhaps threatening or even frightening.

Folk customs and values

Manners are actually expressions of something deeper. They seem simple and not very urgent, yet they are really very important. Manners are folk customs that tell us much about the person who follows them—and just as much about the person who does not.

Folk customs are the expressions of things we believe in

FOLKWAYS AND PATTERNS

The patterns of a folk dance are handed down for generations. A caller calls out the steps for those who need to be reminded. The manners and morals of a group make up folk patterns too. They tell us how to listen, when to smile, how to greet a friend— how to play and work fairly with others.

and things we value. Smiling when we greet someone instead of frowning is more than just being polite. It tells the person we are greeting that we like him, or at least that we are open to the possibility of liking him.

Smiling may feel as if it is automatic, a thing that happens by itself, yet it is not. It requires a choice and a decision. It requires us to change, even if only in a small way. Smiling became our folk custom because we value friendliness.

To see how our values affect us, consider this incident in the life of one of our sages, Simeon ben Shetaḥ.

Simeon was extremely poor. Nor would he accept any money for his teaching—he believed that learning was a gift to him from his teachers, so he made a gift of learning to his students.

Still, he had somehow to earn his daily bread. And this he did by carrying—he carried wood for his neighbors' fires, water for his neighbors' tables. In return, he was able to earn a small sum of money each week.

To ease his burden, his students once bought Simeon a donkey from an Arab in the marketplace. The rabbi was much pleased with his gift.

But as he examined it carefully, he noticed something strange: tied around the donkey's neck was a small leather purse, and inside the purse—a pearl!

"What a great fortune!" the students exclaimed. "Now the rabbi will no longer be poor."

Simeon replied, "This pearl belongs to the man who sold you the donkey."

"But the Arab sold us the whole donkey," the students argued. "And since this pearl was attached to the animal when we bought it, he sold us the pearl as well. We have given it to you. According to the law, you need not return it."

"Of what use is my learning," Simeon asked his students, "if I do not act in the right way?"

Simeon then took the pearl and the purse back to the marketplace. When the Arab saw the pearl, he was dumbfounded. Finally, overcoming his speechless surprise at the pearl's return, he managed to say, "Blessed be the God of Simeon ben Shetaḥ." [Deut. R. 3:3]

The Arab in the story well understood Simeon's actions:

We try to understand the universe. Through the natural sciences we discover the laws of nature. Through moral research we seek out our values. And action reflects what our values are.

Simeon had expressed by deed a moral value. To Simeon this value was more precious than a pearl, more worthwhile than money, and obviously even more important than the mere letter of the law. Simeon had stepped beyond the boundaries of usual action to do something unusual—and unusually praiseworthy.

We learn the values that our group prizes through following the patterns of the group, patterns that are made up of custom and law. Then, when there is no apparent example for a particular case, we make our decision on the basis of what we think the group would find most acceptable. That is what Simeon was doing in the case of the donkey and the pearl. Even though the law did not cover this particular case, Simeon followed the value that the law represented: a Jewish way of thinking which included honesty and the belief that doing what is good for others is good for oneself.

Values and choices

Our values, rituals, and folk customs serve us in three ways. They help us to hold our group together. They keep fighting within our group to a minimum. And they set our group apart from other groups, making it easily identifiable.

Keeping a group together   First, and most importantly, our values and customs hold our group together. Think about your school and its traditions, for example. Your school may have an anthem or "fight song." It may have cheers that it has adopted so that you can root for your teams. There is probably a school spirit based on many small bits and pieces of tradition —the tradition of having a strong basketball team, the feeling of strength gained at a pep rally, or the tradition of high scholastic achievement. All of these things help to make the student body of the school a single, close-knit group. And all these things tend to draw the individuals who go to your school closer together.

If later on in life, you meet others who went to the same school, you probably will feel friendlier toward them than toward a complete stranger—even if you did not know them when you were going to school together.

When people share membership in a group, they feel more comfortable together. This comfort arises out of shared traditions, shared beliefs and values, and shared customs. It gives us a common ground on which to stand.

Keeping peace   The second function of a set of traditions is controlling the fighting wihin a group. Because a group is held together by shared beliefs and feels comfortable together, fighting within is kept to a bare minimum. There can be minor disagreements, of course, but they are more like friendly arguments than battles.

If the group grows too large to be comfortable, it often splits into smaller groups of people with more common interests. The splitting apart can be a painful process. In the history of the United States there was a point at which the values and beliefs of the North and the South differed so much that they were really two groups and no longer one.

Even at the end of the Civil War, the Northerners found it difficult to impose their values on the South, and a long and trying period of adjustment, bitter and hard, was the result. But from within, each group was held together by its separate tradition. And even while the fighting raged

VALUES AND TOGETHERNESS

Membership in a group ties people together in loyalties and traditions. If the shared traditions and values of a group are good, group members are less likely to fight among themselves. Instead, they feel like shouting, "Yea, Team!"

between the two groups, the fighting within each group was kept to a minimum.

So we can see that a strong set of shared beliefs, opinions, values and traditions bind a group into one close-knit unit, and serve to keep the peace from within.

The last function of traditions, values, and customs is to set your group apart from all others. Each group believes that it is unique and personal as long as it has distinct and differing ways of behaving. But you may ask, why should we seek to be different? Aren't we all human beings? Wouldn't there be peace in the world if we could have just one group?

Establishing boundaries

That, indeed, is one of our cherished hopes as Jews— that if we work to bring about a time of peace, the world will be united under the kingship of God alone, and each of us will be free to live without fear of war, crime, poverty, disease, or hunger.

In the end of days it shall come to pass,
That the mountain of the Lord's house shall be
   established as the top of the mountains. . . .
And many nations shall go and say:
"Come ye, and let us go up to the mountain of the Lord,
And to the house of the God of Jacob;
And He will teach us His ways,
And we will walk in His paths." [Mic. 4:1–2]

Until this biblical prophecy has been fulfilled, however, groups still serve a purpose. The traditions and values of the group provide a kind of test for us. They provide goals for us to reach; and they are designed especially to meet our needs in our particular time and place. The needs of people are different in other places around the world. In some ways, they may be different on the next block or in another section of the same city in which we live. A group that took in the whole world could not have full meaning for us and would not really answer our moment to moment needs.

All that establishing boundaries really means is that we come to know where one group ends and another begins. We come to see them as separate and distinct. And we find how each group helps us in its own way.

The Jewish group Of the many groups to which we may belong, the most demanding is the Jewish people. To be a Jew, one must come to know, understand, and live by a great many traditionally Jewish values, values that serve much the same purpose as values in all groups, yet are special and unique to the Jewish people: our values and folk customs are

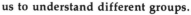

THE NEED FOR BOUNDARIES

At the End of Days all nations shall worship the Lord and walk in His ways. But in the here and now, people of different groups have differing values and customs and manners. These draw boundaries between them. Recognizing these boundaries helps us to understand different groups.

designed to minimize or eliminate feuding, to hold our people close together in spirit no matter how far apart they are in distance, and to separate Jews from other groups in order to insure our survival as a people.

The Jewish tradition is made up of the shared beliefs and values of our people. Yet each new member of the Jewish group must learn this tradition anew, as if uncovering each idea and custom for the first time.

Jewish tradition— our measuring stick

The rabbis of ancient Israel knew this. Most of them were teachers seeking to pass the tradition from their generation to the next. Gathering the greatest teachings of some sixty rabbis who lived from approximately 300 B.C.E. to 200 C.E., the rabbis created a basic textbook of Jewish values, and called it *Pirke Avot (The Sayings of the Fathers)*.

In the search for moral wisdom, the record of achievement contained in Pirke Avot is unique. The teachings and principles still serve today as a measure of our progress toward unity and peace, toward the Days of the Messiah.

We are ever-changing. Our lives are complicated and sometimes difficult; answers are not easily found to the choices we must make. Yet much of our behavior is already patterned: directed by folk customs that express the values of the groups we belong to. Each of these groups builds its own traditions that serve to keep the group together, to reduce fighting within the group to a minimum, and to establish boundaries that mark the group as unique. As a part of your personal process of growth, you will wish to examine the values and traditions you have inherited so that you may choose freely those that are most important for you and those that you will honor because they are important to people you love.

Reflection

In this book we will examine the Jewish tradition, using Pirke Avot as our basis, inquiring into the forms we can call "Jewish action." We shall talk about practical values, about how people change and grow as they respond to the world they live in, with a special emphasis on the world you live in now.

2

Our freedom to choose

Describing yourself   Since this is a book about Jewish values and how they affect you, the place to begin—if the book is going to be of some practical value—is with you. Before you read any further, make a few notes about yourself: on a piece of paper, jot down ten or so phrases that best describe you.

You might say that you are a human being. You might describe yourself as Jewish. You might also say that you are an American: you are a citizen of the United States. You are a resident of a particular state, county, city, and neighborhood. You are a teenager. You are either male or female. You belong to a particular school community. You might describe yourself as happy, sad, thoughtful, or careless. You may be a scout, a member of a ball team, a youth grouper, a club member, a horseback rider, a rightfielder, a tennis buff, and so on.

You and groups   What may surprise you as you look over the list is that the terms that we use to describe ourselves most often have to do with other people, usually with other people in groups.

WHICH GROUP?

Some groups we are born into, while others we choose to join. But what membership in any group means in our lives is largely up to us.

We participate in a great number of groups and groupings. Each group has its own traditions and sets of values.

Some groups we choose because of their traditions and their values. In choosing a synagogue, a youth group, or a club, we consider what it might do for us. We consider, too, whether the people who belong to such groups are the kind of people we would like to be with and share experiences with.

And of course there are many groups that we belong to and have no choice about. For example, you cannot choose whether or not you will be a human being, just as you cannot choose whether you will be male or female. You do not choose your family group, either.

Yet all of the groups to which we belong, whether by chance or by choice, affect us and influence the way we act and the way we think.

As we saw in the first chapter, groups operate to protect themselves. As members of a group, we seek to establish

Traditions in conflict

boundaries between ourselves and other groups (these boundaries are usually sets of common beliefs and actions), we try to keep the group together, and we try to keep harmony within the group by maintaining common traditions.

Every group to which we belong is, in a way, in competition with every other group. Each group wants our undivided loyalty; each group wants us to believe as much as possible in the values and traditions it holds as a group. We are pulled in many directions at once.

Yet this is good. Though choosing between groups may sometimes be painful, it is better than not being able to choose at all. It is one of the blessings we share that we are able to think, to study, to judge, to choose, and to act freely.

Because we live in a complex society, we are constantly faced with decisions of preference. We have to make choices because we have so many interests. Should you attend the regular meeting of your math club after school on Thursday, or should you skip it in order to represent your class in a swim meet? Should you study alone, or join a group of friends for a game of soccer? Still, it is much better to have varied interests, and we are lucky to have reasons for choosing and the freedom to act.

MY DIME AND I

Just standing before a vending machine can give us pause. How much more, then, when we must choose between traditions: going to synagogue on Friday night or marching in the school band?

Yes or no, here or there,
this or that, red or blue,
Study or play, art or math,
love or hate, life or death...

Imagine that you had been born instead into a life of slavery some time before the Civil War. Your father was a slave and so was your mother. You could only look forward to the day when your children would be slaves, too. You would be the property of your master, to be sold or bought at his whim, separated from family or friends, even from wife or husband.

Mostly, you would be faced with a life of labor. If you were strong, you would labor in the fields twelve or fourteen hours a day, perhaps picking cotton or raising vegetables. If you were weak, or smart, you might become a household servant or a stable hand. But weaker or stronger, smarter or slower, your future would be the same, made up of days that resembled the present, which was totally like the past.

If the master was kindly, the picture might be a little brighter—perhaps you would not be worked to death, perhaps in your last years you could retire to just shining shoes or brushing down sweaty horses.

But for the most part, slavery in the United States was monotonous. Slaves could make no real choices, with a few exceptions—and those few exceptions could always be changed at the master's whim.

Being free to make choices gives life meaning. As opposed to the life of the slave, the Jewish tradition has always taught us to choose freedom and free choice. This value of freedom is seen very clearly in what we call the Oral Tradition. The sages and rabbis of the Second Commonwealth taught that the Oral Tradition had been given at Mount Sinai along with the Written Tradition, the Torah. It had been passed on from generation to generation, from parent to child, until the rabbis decided to record it in the Talmud. In Pirke Avot we read:

To give life meaning

> *Moses received the Torah [in other words, the Oral Tradition] on Sinai, and handed it down to Joshua; Joshua to the elders; the elders to the prophets; and the prophets handed it down to the Men of the Great Assembly. [Avot 1:1]*

One book in particular has become representative of the rabbinic tradition—Pirke Avot.

Everything found in Pirke Avot is based on the teaching of the rabbis that a person must choose freedom over slavery. The rabbis pointed out that life without freedom of choice is merely senseless slavery—the kind of slavery that is found among drones in a beehive.

An interesting way of explaining our need for inner freedom is found in a later, mystical work, the Zohar:

Before creating this world, God created many others without the Torah. Because He had created them, each of these worlds was perfect, each of them beautiful—but they were meaningless worlds because they were static and did not grow or change. In these previous worlds there was no lust, but there was no love, either. There was no cruelty, but there was no compassion, either. There was perfect satisfaction, but there was no ambition. There was no strife, but no peace. There was no sorrow, but no joy, either. Everything was without flaw, but there was no hope of anything becoming better.

The real spark of life—freedom, free will, the chance and ability to choose good from evil, to sin with a chance to repent, the ability to create or to fail—these were missing.

This world, which God created using the Torah as His plan, is a dynamic world, a world in which man can choose. [Zoh. 1:24b]

The noble flaw In creating a world in which men and women could have choices and decisions to make, God had to allow for a world that would be less than perfect. This is the rabbinic view—that in order to allow for freedom and free will, God had to allow for the presence of evil.

Other religions and philosophies have offered different reasons for the existence of evil in the world. The Catholic Church, for example, believes that everyone is born in a state of sin and must seek redemption from it. Puritans believed that only a few people were chosen to enter heaven when they died. They inclined to believe that these "elect" were probably those who were the most hardworking, successful, and prosperous in this life. Still, one could not be sure of election or salvation. Buddhism sees the material world as filled with evil. According to the teachings of the Buddha, life in this world is a wheel of

WHAT WOULD I DO?

Have you ever wished for a perfect world, one with no flaws or faults? One in which you had just everything? What do you imagine it might be like?

suffering that we can escape only by continued inner concentration.

According to the ancient Greeks, no religion, no person could control good and evil within his life. Fate and chance ruled the world, doing as they pleased, and an unhappy or wronged god or goddess could ruin a person's life for no apparent reason.

Taoists came to believe that the world and its forces are

ruled by two powers, good and evil, which are the same as light and darkness. According to the philosophy of Taoism, there is little reason to hope that good will finally triumph.

In contrast, the rabbis saw a possibility for the earth and all its inhabitants to arrive at a time of peace and good. They spoke of this time as the Days of the Messiah, the World to Come and the End of Days. But whatever name they called it, they clearly meant that it would be a time of peace in this life, not in some heaven or afterlife. Bringing about this time of peace requires effort on the part of each and every person; and it requires an understanding of God's law, the Torah. For it is the law that helps us to control evil in our world.

Reflection   In order to give life meaning, God has created a world in which evil is a *possibility*. The word *possibility* is crucial. People are not born evil in our view, they are born with a possibility of doing evil. But even doing evil does not mean that a person *is* evil—all of us miss the mark from time to time, making a mistake or falling short of our potential for good.

Unlike other religions and philosophies, Judaism teaches that the world holds the possibilities for both evil and good, as well as the most important possibility of all—the possibility for change. We Jews see the world not as a place of suffering only, but as a place that can be transformed through our work into a new Garden of Eden. This is the rabbinic idea. "Sin crouches at the door awaiting, and wishes you to choose it—but you may rule over it" [Gen. 4:7]. Evil is not a necessity, but only one of two alternatives.

3

The struggle within us

In making choices, the rabbis believed, two forces are at work within us. One of these is our desire to do what is good, the other our desire to do what is evil.

The rabbis called the impulse or inclination to do what is good the *Yetzer Tov*. *Yetzer* is the Hebrew word for "impulse," *Tov* the Hebrew word for "good."

The other impulse, the inclination to do what is evil, they named the *Yetzer HaRa*. The word *Ra* is Hebrew for "evil."

The kind of a person each of us is depends on how we handle these two impulses. The Yetzer Tov controls the righteous person, while the Yetzer HaRa is in control of the wicked. The Talmud says, however, that *"both* impulses control the average person" [Ber. 61a]. Most of us fit into this last category, being neither totally good nor totally wicked.

The forces within us

יצר טוב

יצר הרע

The Yetzer Tov, or impulse for good, pulls us in one direction. The Yetzer HaRa, or impulse to evil or selfishness, pulls us in another. Most of us are pulled back and forth at times between the desire to be good and the desire to be selfish—or at least to have our own way.

Needing impulses for both right and wrong

But how do we judge what is right and what is wrong? How can we tell one impulse from another? The choice is not always a clear one. Aren't the rabbis oversimplifying when they imply that there is always an "evil" choice and always a "good" one?

The rabbis' understanding was actually much more complex. They did not believe that the Yetzer HaRa *is* evil—it is just an *inclination toward* evil, a leaning in the direction of evil. They even saw that it could be helpful in many ways.

To show how this might be so, they told this parable:

Our sages once caught the Yetzer HaRa and bound it up with golden chains. At first they were very pleased with themselves. Thievery stopped, murder ceased. People were all friendly and loving toward one another. There was no jealousy, and in all of Israel no arguments occurred between an Israelite and a neighbor. No one died.

But suddenly they began to see a strange thing happening. People were so content that they did not bother to toil. There was no competition, so people quit working. No new houses were built. People no longer married or wanted to have children. Even the rabbis began to turn to laziness.

Then the rabbis understood how important the Yetzer HaRa was to the world. So they broke the chains that bound it and set it free.
[Gen. R. 9:7]

The easiest way to understand the Yetzer HaRa is to see it as extreme selfishness. It is the part of us that is always claiming that things are "mine," or calling out, "I want . . ." or "Gimme . . ." What makes it dangerous is that it comes to control us if we do not balance it and control it.

The Yetzer HaRa may begin to take hold by asking us to do a small thing such as taking a book and not returning it. Soon it requires us to do something worse. It may say to us, "Just do this one time—it cannot hurt anyone if you only do it one time." Then soon it requires us to do evil all the time: "Come and hurt this one. Look how weak he is: he cannot hurt you in return."

At first, the Yetzer HaRa is like a spider's web, but in the end it is like heavy ropes. At first, the Yetzer is like a passerby, then it is like a guest, and finally it becomes the master of the house. At first, the Yetzer is sweet; in the end it is bitter [Suk. 52a; Suk. 52b; Jerus. T., Shab. 14c].

Controlling selfishness is not always easy. The more we allow ourselves to be selfish, the more selfish we become. Then we actually lose our ability to choose and begin to act

Selfishness

A formula

KEEPING OUR BALANCE

To be totally selfish would be bad for others. To be overly good and totally unselfish could be harmful to ourselves—and perhaps to others, too! To stay on the beam we must strike a balance between the Yetzer Tov and the Yetzer HaRa.

always for ourselves alone. We give up our freedom, our free will, and trade it for whatever we feel like doing at the moment, which is only the illusion of freedom.

This might be all right if we did not have to live with other people. But if you look back at the list you were asked to prepare at the beginning of Chapter 2, you must see that most of your life is built around others and around the groups of people to which you belong.

So we must learn to seek some kind of a balance. It is not *always* wrong to be selfish, but it cannot always be *right*, either. It is not *always* good to share all things, but it cannot always be *wrong*, either. Somewhere in between is a path worth following.

Here we may take a lesson from Hillel, the great teacher of Mishnaic times. In the way he lived and the teachings he passed on, Hillel sought a formula for making intelligent choices. He summarized his formula in Pirke Avot:

אִם אֵין אֲנִי לִי מִי לִי. וּכְשֶׁאֲנִי לְעַצְמִי מָה אָנִי. וְאִם לֹא
עַכְשָׁו אֵימָתָי:

"If I am not for myself, who will be for me? And if I am only for myself, what am I? And if not now, when?" [Avot 1:14]

"If I am not for myself . . ." If you are to take an active part in the world in which you live, you must stand for something. You must come to have some understanding of the things you are, the things you want to have, the things you want to be, the things you are willing to work for, the things that you care about. In other words, you must start with yourself.

Not everything that you want for yourself is selfish. But almost anything that you want for yourself *alone,* or only for your sake is selfish. You may wish to gain knowledge. By itself, that is not selfish. A knowledgeable person is of more use to the world than one who is ignorant. But if you use your knowledge to hurt others, or only for your own sake, then you are being selfish in a harmful way.

You may wish to be popular. That is not selfish. A

popular person can help neighbors by bringing them closer together, by settling arguments and disputes, by being kind and understanding. But when a popular person turns his talent to leading people in evil directions, he is giving way to the Yetzer HaRa. In using his popularity to lead his people into war after war, Napoleon harmed the French people instead of helping them.

You may wish to be wealthy. That in itself is not selfish. A wealthy person can help others, using his wealth to benefit those who are in need; a wealthy person may also be a blessing to the community by sponsoring noble works and actions. But if a person wishes to be wealthy at the expense of others, then that is an example of Yetzer HaRa acting through sheer selfishness.

Hillel's first question, "If I am not for myself, who will be for me?" implies that a person should strive to help himself. You should labor to be what you want to be, you should labor to be better—for if you do not work for yourself, who will do it for you?

"If I am only for myself . . ."

But if all your labors are for yourself alone, what good are you? Always we come back to this: that there is more in your life than you alone. Your life begins to have real meaning only when you begin to choose ways and means of working that are considerate of others.

If you lived totally alone, how you behaved would make no difference to anyone—perhaps even to yourself. That is why Hillel's second question—"If I am only for myself, what am I?—is so important. Living with others means that we must consider their needs and wants, even as we consider our own.

The Yetzer HaRa would like us always to be for ourselves alone. It wants us to ask Hillel's first question in a slightly different way: "If I don't get such and such for myself, who else will get it for me?" But Hillel brings the matter into proper balance when he continues his questioning: his second question asks, in effect, "If I get such and such at someone else's expense or harm, am I not evil?" Hillel could see that the Yetzer HaRa is important, but that the two urges must be balanced. Only in that way could a person best serve his community and, in the end, himself.

"If not now, when?" The last part of Hillel's three-part question is equally important: "If not now, when?"

We are human; all of us enjoy putting things off until tomorrow. Yet if we never begin, or if we say, "I will let myself do evil just this one time," we become slaves. We lose our freedom to choose.

Some of us suffer from too much selfishness. Others may suffer from too much self-*less*-ness: they may think too little of themselves. If we do not seek to bring about a balance in our lives, we can hope only for a kind of laziness to set in, a resistance to change and progress, perhaps a fear of trying something new, or of trying to make our lives better and richer.

There is only one cure for this, Hillel implies. Act now! Do not wait until tomorrow. Do not say, "Tomorrow I will begin." Begin immediately!

The Time is NOW
NOW NOW
now

THE WHY AND WHEN OF IT ALL

What do I want things for? Skill? Knowledge? Wisdom? Popularity? Strength? Prosperity? Can I use these good things for others as well as for myself? And when do I set about beginning? If my motive is right, the time is now.

This book is built around the three questions of Hillel found in Pirke Avot:

If I am not for myself, who will be for me? And if I am only for myself, what am I? And if not now, when?

In the first unit of this book—these first three chapters and the following one—we consider the problem of preparing ourselves for action. In the second unit—chapters 5–11—we will speak of the kinds of choices that each of us must make in life, for his own sake. In the third unit—chapters 12–22—we will speak of the kind of choices we must make if we are to live well together in our community. And in the last unit—chapters 22 and 23—we speak of what we must do immediately to set our course and set it rightly.

Always our studies will lead us back to these ideas: that each of us is a complex and complicated being, one who is unique and singular; that every one of us inwardly struggles between what is good and what is evil, as well as between what is right for ourselves and what is right for the world in which we live; that this struggle gives meaning to our lives and to the world around us; and that the success of this struggle finally depends on how well we balance the worst and the best of what is within ourselves and in the world.

In order to throw light on our struggle and to help us interpret the complexity of the world, we shall draw upon our own tradition—the rabbinic point of view, which holds that evil may be overcome through proper action and proper thought and that the Yetzer HaRa, the impulse to do what is evil, may be turned to good. We shall even examine the actions, words, and thoughts of the rabbis themselves to see how their principles fared in practice.

Remember the choice between good and evil is always yours to make, for freedom of choice is your Jewish heritage and your birthright as a human being. Choosing well, then, is finally your personal responsibility.

4

Our tradition and Pirke Avot

The way of flesh Judaism is a complex web of ideas and concepts, commandments and commentaries. At first, you may stand bewildered and say, "Is there a beginning to all this?"

The answer may very well be a firm no. The rabbis claimed that even before the Torah, there was *derech eretz*, which means "the way the world goes."

> *Without the Torah, we could have learned modesty from the cat, honesty from the ant, purity from the dove, and good manners from the rooster.* [Erub. 100b]

דרך ארץ   But derech eretz was not enough. Cats might teach modesty in many ways, but they also teach cruelty. And while it is true that ants will not steal from one another, as a group they steal from other creatures whatever they can. Nature is not a good teacher of morals.

The Tanach With the Torah a new light dawned for the history of moral behavior. The Torah, the Five Books of Moses, provides for the Jewish people a source for studying the ways of the world and the requirements of the Lord who created it. These requirements we call מִצְוֹת commandments.

The rabbis taught that there are 613 commandments (*mitzvot*) to be found in the Torah. Of these 613 mitzvot, 248 are positive in nature. (An example is the mitzvah, *"Hear, O Israel, the Lord is our God, the Lord is One"* [Deut. 6:4].) The remaining 365 are negatively phrased mitzvot (for example, *"Do not join hands with the wicked"* [Exod. 23:1]). At first glance, fulfilling all 613 commandments seems like an overwhelming task. But once a person continues looking for ways to follow the path of Torah, the path soon becomes worthwhile, even if it is not always easy.

At a later time, two great bodies of work were added to the Torah. The first of these is called נְבִיאִים, Prophets, which contains the history of the Judges and early Prophets, the history of the kingdoms of Israel and Judah, the works of the twelve minor Prophets, and the works of three major Prophets—Isaiah, Jeremiah, and Ezekiel.

The second collection to be added to the Torah is called כְּתוּבִים, Writings, made up of poetry, proverbs, and stories of wisdom, as well as three historical books—Ezra, Nehemiah, and Chronicles.

THE BIBLE—TANACH

Tanach is the acronym for the three parts of the Bible —first the Torah, or five books of Moses, with the 613 commandments; then the Prophets, including the history of the early Prophets and Judges; and finally the Writings, comprising poetry, stories of wisdom, proverbs, and history.

This whole vast body of literature we call in English the Bible. In Hebrew it is known by an acronym—a name made up of the first letter of each of its three parts. The three parts are תּוֹרָה , נְבִיאִים , and כְּתוּבִים and the acronym is תַּנַ"ךְ , *Tanach*. (In the world of Jewish study many names are made up in this way.)

The Mishnah At the beginning of the third century C.E., Rabbi Yehudah HaNasi and his colleagues compiled and edited a collection of Jewish law, learning, and ethics called the *Mishnah*.

THE MISHNAH

The Mishnah was first preserved as the Oral Tradition, and even though it is now in written form, we still call it the Oral Law. It represents the work of early teachers, the Tannaim. It was compiled and edited at the beginning of the third century C.E.

Before this time, the Mishnah had existed in other forms. At first, it was passed down from teacher to student by word of mouth; and so it became known as the Oral Law or Oral Tradition. It was probably Hillel who later gave the Oral Law its first written form so that it could be used by him as a textbook.

As it exists today, the Mishnah contains six *sedarim* (orders): *Zeraim, Moed, Nashim, Nezikin, Kodashim,* and *Tohorot.* Each order is in turn subdivided into short books called *tractates.*

Zeraim (Seeds) contains eleven tractates dealing with agriculture and prayer.

Moed (Seasons) contains twelve tractates dealing with the festivals and how we are to observe them.

Nashim (Women) contains seven tractates on the laws concerning marriage and divorce.

Nezikin (Damages) contains ten tractates on civil laws and the laws of punishment.

Kodashim (Sacred Things) contains eleven tractates on the laws of sacrifice in the ancient Temple in Jerusalem.

Tohorot (Cleanliness) contains twelve tractates on the laws of ritual purity.

The idea behind compiling the Mishnah was to give Jews a guide for following the 613 mitzvot of the Torah in their daily lives.

The Talmud

The teachers who lived after the time of Hillel and Shammai and whose work is compiled in the Mishnah were called *Tannaim,* from the Aramaic word meaning "to teach." The Tannaim, whose work completed the Mishnah, had followers called *Amoraim,* meaning "interpreters." The Amoraim were in turn responsible for a collection of commentaries on the Mishnah called the *Gemara* (from the Aramaic word "to learn"). You might ask, since the Mishnah is already a working out of the laws of the Torah, why should we need the Gemara, which is a working out of the laws of the Mishnah?

The reason for needing both the Mishnah *and* the Gemara is that they each reflect Judaism passing through im-

The Amoraim added a commentary to the Mishnah, called the Gemara. As the Mishnah served to explain the mitzvot, so the Gemara helped to explain the Mishnah. Together, Mishnah and Gemara make up the Talmud.

portant stages in the process of growth and change. As the laws were taught and discussed, they were continually being viewed in new ways and being applied to new situations and problems in the life of the Jewish people.

Together, the Mishnah and the Gemara make up what we call the *Talmud*. Actually, since there were Amoraim writing both in Palestine and Babylonia, there are two such works: the Palestinian or Jerusalem Talmud and the Babylonian Talmud. The Babylonian Talmud, however, is by far the greater in most respects. In size alone, it is four times larger than the Jerusalem Talmud. The Babylonian Talmud, then, is usually what is meant when we speak of *the* Talmud.

Commentary upon commentary As time went on, other commentaries were written on the Bible and even on the Talmud itself. Probably the most famous commentator of all time is Rashi of Troyes (1040–1105). The name Rashi is an acronym for *Ra*bbi *Sh*lomo *Yi*tzḥaki. Rashi set for himself the task of making the Bible and the Talmud less difficult for the Jews of his time. He wrote in a Hebrew style that was clear and extremely simple; when he could not find a simple Hebrew word that expressed exactly what he wanted to say for example, he would include a word or two of French. It is fitting that Rashi's commentary on the Torah was the first book written in Hebrew to be printed (1475) using the modern system of movable type.

Other great commentators include Rabbi Abraham ibn Ezra (1092–1167), a great poet and traveler; Rabbi Shmuel ben Meir, called the Rashbam (1085–1174), Rashi's grandson (whose comments often disagreed with the interpretations of his famous grandfather); and Rabbi Moshe ben Nahman, called Ramban (1194–1270), who was also known as Nahmanides, who was a great admirer of Maimonides.

The list continues down to the present day, for even now commentaries are being written on the Bible and on the Talmud.

And more

There are many other collections and works commenting on the Bible and the Talmud that we have not mentioned: the Midrash, a collection of folklore and commentary arranged around biblical verses; the Tosefta, a collection of laws very similar to those in the Mishnah; the Apocrypha, a collection of writings from around the same time as those in the Tanach but not included along with them—and more.

Pirke Avot

פרקי
אבות

It seems amazing that one small tractate of six chapters from the Mishnah can sum up the ethical teachings of this vast network of folklore, law, legend, and the Bible. But then, Pirke Avot is an amazing book. It comes from the Seder Nezikin, in which it is the ninth tractate. But very early it was adopted as a regular part of the study materials for Shabbat, and so it was included in the prayer book. In the Mishnah, Pirke Avot (or Avot, for short) has only five chapters, but when it became a regular part of the prayer service a sixth Perek (chapter) was added.

Avot is made up of the sayings of some sixty rabbis, extending over a period of nearly 500 years, roughly from 300 B.C.E. to 200 C.E. Every one of the sayings is a brief summary of all or part of the teachings of one of these rabbis. And almost every saying is concerned with the way we treat one another in our daily lives—our moral conduct.

Pirke Avot and politics

Some historians have claimed that Pirke Avot was originally collected for political reasons—that it was put to-

Pirke Avot, the Sayings of the Fathers, is taken from
Seder Nezikin ("Damages")—an order of the
Mishnah—in which it is the ninth tractate. In the
traditional prayerbook, Avot has six chapters instead
of the original five.

gether by a group of sages known as the Pharisees in order
to prove that theirs was the true tradition of Judaism.

But whether or not this was its original intention, Pirke
Avot has come to mean a great deal more than that to the
Jewish people. Its sayings and advice are still fresh and
useful today. If anything, they have grown more important, for as we read them we can see in them the mark of
eternal truths. True, some are so outdated as to be beyond
repair, others the product of ancient superstitions, and still
others merely folklore inserted as if by accident. For the
most part, however, the words and teachings that make up
Pirke Avot have become part of both Jewish speech and
Jewish life.

**Pirke Avot and
the tradition**
In the first three chapters of this book we spoke about the
use of tradition in sustaining the group. Pirke Avot serves
as the spokesman for our Jewish tradition. It is a collection
of much of the best moral teachings of our people, a key to
observing the mitzvot of the Torah in our everyday lives.

Then, too, almost no other book in the literature of
Judaism has been the focus of so many commentators as
Pirke Avot. In fact, whenever a person opens Pirke Avot
for the first time, he or she begins a new commentary—a
personal commentary. Everyone who studies Avot brings
to it new ideas and new applications, for each of us is
unique and no two of us think alike.

One reason why Pirke Avot, the entire Talmud, the Tanach, and the myriad other works of Jewish wisdom have been preserved with such great dedication is in order to give you a chance to encounter them personally. By reading them with your own eyes, by applying your own ideas, your own mind, in your special place in time, you can study them, comment on them, react to them, come to know and cherish them, and pass them on to your children as a precious heritage.

In our study this year of how Jews act, we will use Pirke Avot as the spokesman for our tradition. Although we will call other witnesses to the stand from time to time, we will concentrate on questioning and cross-examining the sixty rabbis whose sayings are recorded in Avot—trying always to expand what they can possibly mean to our modern world. Such a study is certainly one worth making, so let us begin by repeating the famous third question posed by Hillel: "If not now, when?"

One master taught:

Every person must have two pockets.

In one pocket should be a piece of paper saying, "I am but dust and ashes." When a person is feeling too proud, he should reach into this pocket and withdraw the paper to read it.

In the other pocket should be a piece of paper saying, "For my sake the world was created." When a person is feeling disheartened and lowly, he should reach into this pocket, withdraw the paper, and read it.

For each of us is the joining together of two worlds. Of clay we are fashioned, but our spirit is the breath of God. We must seek to balance in our lives what is ordinary and what is holy, what is creaturely and what is sacred.

5

The value of life

Just what is the value of a single human life? How much do you think *you* are worth? Some scientist not too long ago added up the value of all the chemicals in the average adult's body and found them to be worth about four dollars.

Judging how much a human being is worth depends to a great extent upon the group doing the judging. Of course, the scientist would certainly agree that a person is worth much more than simply the total money value of the chemicals in his body. In fact, the modern view of the importance of each person—as an individual with a part to play in this world and a share in the future—is very much a result of the heritage of Judaism.

Our group and our values

Judaism teaches us the essential value and importance of each and every human being. The rabbis saw each person as a precious commodity, totally irreplaceable: they taught that "one person is equal to the whole of Creation" [ARN 31].

Man was first created a single individual to teach the lesson that whoever destroys one life, Scripture ascribes it to him as though he had destroyed a whole world; and whoever saves one life, Scripture ascribes it to him as though he had saved a whole world. [Mishnah, Sanh. 4:5]

The image of God   At the heart of this idea of the worth of the individual is the Jewish teaching that the human being is created in the image of God. This first occurs in the book of Genesis, in the story of Creation:

And God said: "Let us make man in our own image, after our likeness; and let them have dominion over the fish of the sea, and over the fowl of the air, and over the cattle, and over all the earth, and over every creeping thing that creepeth upon the earth." And God created man in His own image, in the image of God created He him; male and female created He them. [Gen. 1:24–27]

The Torah here assumes that from the very beginning of time there was within each individual some element that resembles the Lord, our Maker. But this is true also of the animals that roam the fields, the birds that inhabit the air, and the fishes that swim in the seas. In what way, then, is the human being unique?

Rabbi Akiba, in Pirke Avot, addressed himself to this very question. Here is his answer:

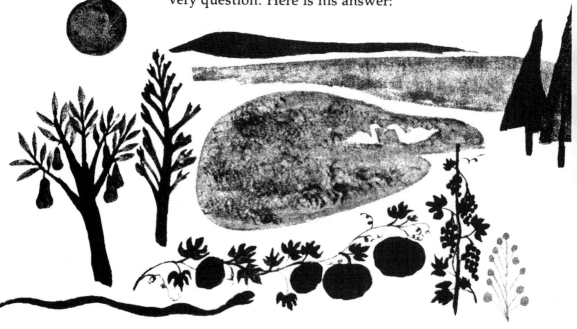

חָבִיב אָדָם שֶׁנִּבְרָא בְצֶלֶם. חִבָּה יְתֵרָה נוֹדַעַת לוֹ שֶׁנִּבְרָא
בְצֶלֶם.

*Beloved is man, for he was created in the image of God; but it was
by a special love that it was made known to him that he was created
in the image of God. [Avot 3:18]*

You may ask, does the Torah mean that we are created in
the *physical* image of God? Is it our bodies to which the
word *image* refers?

The answer is twofold. First, we may observe that
human beings are by no means all alike: we are not all
physically the same. In size we range from dwarfish to
gigantic. In color, from ebony through red and yellow to
white albino. And we differ, too, in sex, posture, strength,
and various abilities. Even our minds, which we must
remember are also basically a physical feature, vary
greatly.

And the Torah goes on to provide us with a second
picture of the creation of humanity, a picture more easily
understandable in human terms than the first, more ele-
vated idea of the "image of God":

MAN IN GOD'S IMAGE

Every human life is precious. God created man in
His own image and likeness. Each of us has a spark
of the divine within. Each can learn to recognize it.

Then the Lord God formed man of the dust of the ground, and breathed into his nostrils the breath of life; and man became a living soul. [Gen. 2:7]

Man the mixture   A new element has been added to the picture. Each of us is a "living soul." It is this soul that makes us different, that sets us apart from the rest of the animal kingdom. The Jewish idea of the soul is not that it is separate from the body. We understand that the soul and the body *together* are the mark of life. It is the soul that understands that the human being is created in the image of God. It is the soul within us which provides the still, small voice of conscience to be heard.

All creatures that are formed of heaven, both their soul and body are heavenly; and all creatures that are formed of earth, both their soul and body are earthbound, with the exception of mankind, whose soul is from heaven and his body is from earth.

Therefore, if a man obeys the Torah and does the will of his Father in heaven, behold he is like the creatures above; as it is written: "I have said, You are gods, and all of you sons of the Most High."

But if he obey not the Torah and perform not the will of his Father in heaven, he is like the creatures below; as it is said: "Nevertheless, you shall die like men." [Sifre Deut. 306:132a]

To live   This special Jewish view of humanity's place in relation to
with dignity   God gives us a special attitude. We do not have to see ourselves as less so that God can be more. We can see each individual as important and vital to the universe, and still God is glorious and supreme over all.

BODY AND SOUL

Our soul is from Heaven, our body from earth.
Through obedience to Torah we gain dignity.
When we obey the Torah we walk with the Most High. When we do not obey, we walk only in the ways of mortals.

46   *If I am not for myself . . .*

As human beings, God has granted us dignity. Perhaps the greatest expression of this is found in the Psalms:

When I behold Your heavens, the work of Your fingers,
The moon and the stars, which You have established;
What is man, that You are mindful of him?
And the son of man, that You think of him?

Yet you have made man but little lower than the angels,
And have crowned him with glory and honor.
You have caused him to rule over the works of Your hands;
You have put all things beneath his feet. [Psalms 8:4–7]

As yourself

So much of Jewish ethics is based on this idea of the dignity of each human being, and the need of each of us to respect it, that we should examine it carefully to understand precisely what is being said.

In a famous story from the Talmud, a nonbeliever challenged Hillel to explain the Torah while standing balanced on one foot. Hillel replied that the essence of the entire Torah is "Do not unto thy fellow men what is hateful to thee—the rest," Hillel said, "is commentary." He then directed the nonbeliever to "go and study."

Hillel's admonition is another way of saying, "Love your neighbor as yourself." And the rabbis pointed out that you cannot truly love your neighbor, unless you first learn to love yourself. For how can you love your neighbor as yourself, if you do not love yourself first?

Only if each of us understands our own importance to the universe, his or her individual worth within the scheme of time and place, can we truly begin to love our neighbors.

How does this work? Imagine that you see a person lying on the sidewalk as you are walking down the road. He is doubled over and holding his stomach. He is moaning and groaning. His body is writhing. What do you think as you see this?

Do you imagine that he is practicing for a future as a snake? Do you imagine that he is searching for a nickel he dropped? Do you imagine that he is having fun examining the sidewalk? Of course not. You know that he is in pain. You even sense it is his stomach that is aching so fiercely.

But how do you know this to be true? Why are you so sure about what is happening? Is it not because you yourself have felt the pain in an aching stomach? And even if your stomach has almost always been healthy, is it not because you ask yourself, how would I come to be in such a position?

Psychologists say that this is reasoning using a "point of reference." We use our experiences, our past feelings, thoughts, and emotions, as points of reference for understanding the feelings, thoughts, and emotions of others. You therefore understand others more as you come to understand yourself more. (And you understand yourself better by studying others, too.)

In saying that you must love yourself before you can truly love others, the rabbis were saying that love must have a point of reference. It must be grounded in the experience you share with others.

Me first   Imagine this situation:

> *Two men have been traveling through a desert. Man A has a flask of water. Man B does not. Both men are dying of thirst.*
>
> *If Man A were to drink the water in his flask, he might be able to reach the town at the desert's edge. On the other hand, if the men were to share the water, neither would reach the town and both would die.*
>
> *Should Man A drink the water? Or should he share it with Man B? What is your opinion?* [Sifra Lev. 25:36]

Our tradition records that this story was given by Ben Petura, one of the sages, as a way of asking the question "Whose life comes first when only one may be saved?"

Two answers are recorded—one given by Ben Petura himself, the other given by Akiba.

Ben Petura said that the two men should share the flask of water. The central question, Ben Petura argued, is not really "Who shall live?" but "What is the right thing to do

normally?" And normally, he said, any of us would share water with another person.

A very interesting thing about this argument is that Ben Petura, who said that the two men should share the water, did not say that Man *A* should give the water to Man *B*. Why? The reason is simple, really. Jewish law requires equal treatment for all. If the law requires Man *A* to give the water to Man *B*, Man *B* would in turn be required to give the water back to Man *A*, and so they would die together in the desert, passing the flask of water back and forth between them.

But Rabbi Akiba disagreed with regard to sharing the water. Akiba argued that it is better to have one dead than two. Therefore, the man who owns the water must drink alone. Later Jewish thinking follows the decision of Akiba.

We are required to consider ourselves first—to respect ourselves first; to love ourselves first.

Much of this is common sense. Even if it were not the Jewish way to save ourselves first, it would still be the most human thing to do in a crisis. That much is common ground, a common point of reference, between the rabbis and us.

Common sense

Yet we repeatedly hear of people who endanger themselves greatly in rescuing or trying to rescue others. Is this not also a Jewish way to act? Again, the answer is based on common sense and a common point of reference: it *is* a Jewish way to act. It is the essence of the full command to "love your neighbor as yourself."

That is, just as you would try to escape from a blazing building in order to save yourself, or try to swim to shore from a shipwreck in order to save yourself, so too you are required to help others in similar situations to save themselves.

But even this requirement cannot be taken too far. We should always seek a middle ground. For example, it does no one any good if you keep giving everything you earn to charity and as a result become so poor that you need charity yourself.

Self-interest or selfishness? This leads us to the difference between pure selfishness—which we have come to see as the Yetzer HaRa, the inclination to do what is evil—and self-interest, which can often be noble and good.

A Hassidic tale illustrates a noble self-interest as follows:

A man came to the rebbe and asked the rebbe to pray for him. (This was a common practice among eastern European Hassidim. These

LOVING OURSELVES AND OTHERS

We are taught to love others as we love ourselves.
So we must first rightly value and love ourselves.
We must first make our own lives strong and good.
Then we can reach out to help those around us.

simple but pious people felt that the rebbe's words would be accepted readily by God, because the rebbe seemed so close to God.)

"Very well," said the rebbe, "and what shall I ask of God?"

"Pray that my son may become a learned man," said the Hassid.

"No," replied the rebbe. "Pray instead that you will become a learned man. Then you will educate your son and the prayer will come true for you and for your son."

Noble self-interest has become such a traditional Jewish value that we constantly see instances of it in the prayerbook used in daily prayer services. For example, in the Amidah, we pray:

You who favor mankind with knowledge and teach mortals understanding, favor us with knowledge, understanding, and discernment from You. We praise You, O Lord, gracious Giver of knowledge. [Siddur]

From its placement in the prayer service, we can understand that the knowledge that we are asking for is a better understanding of our relationship with God—that is why we say "knowledge, understanding, and discernment *from You.*" The deeper meaning of life can be found only when God grants us the gift of knowledge that only He can give us.

Why? Which finally brings us to the most essential question of all: Why should there be such a thing as a being with a soul, a being that aspires for things to be better, a being with an imagination and a will, a being that searches, a being that questions? Why should there be human existence at all?

The rabbis gave us a twofold reason for the existence of this special dignified being that we call the human being: first, it is the task of the human being to delight God, and second, it is our task to weave the cloth of righteousness.

To delight the Lord A saying has it that "God created man because He loved stories." And the last sentence of Pirke Avot, too, dwells on this idea of God's delight in His creation:

כֹּל מַה שֶּׁבָּרָא הַקָּדוֹשׁ בָּרוּךְ הוּא בְּעוֹלָמוֹ. לֹא בְרָאוֹ אֶלָּא לִכְבוֹדוֹ.

Whatsoever the Holy One, blessed be He, created in His world, He created it but for His glory. [Avot 6:11]

Rabbi Aibu is quoted as having told the following parable:

When God created man, He did so with great care. First, he created man's food needs, and only then did God create mankind.

Nevertheless, the angels complained, using the words of the Psalms: "What is man that You are mindful of him, and the son of man, that You think of him?" [Psalms 8:5]. "This trouble," they went on, "for what purpose have You created it?"

Then God replied, "I have designed a palace and filled it with all things good. But what pleasure have I in this palace full of goodly things with no guests?"

Then the Angels replied, "Sovereign of the Universe! Do what pleases You." [Gen. R. 8:6]

FOR PRAISE AND GLORY

For the glory and praise of God all things were created. Humanity delights in the world. And God delights in humanity and in all His creation.

Of course, the rabbis understood this delight that God has in the world to be based on His love for mankind. In the same way, we should strive to delight in the good things of life: "A person will have to give account on Judgment Day for every good thing which his eyes saw and he did not sample" [Jerus. T., Kid. 4]

In any case, spending our whole lives working for possessions can hardly be seen as worthwhile. As it is written in the Book of Ecclesiastes, when man leaves this world he "shall take nothing for his labor that he may carry away in his hand" [Eccles. 5:15].

When we look at the world from this point of view, it seems a hopeless place indeed. The child is born wanting things—at first, love and food, soon possessions and pleasures. And when one dies he leaves behind everything for which he worked.

The way of the world

A certain king of Adiabene, Monobazus, who lived in the first century C.E., became a convert to Judaism. During a great famine in his land, he gave away all his wealth to the poor so that they might buy food.

His relatives came to him and called him foolish. But he replied, "My ancestors stored up treasures for below. I have stored my treasures for above. They stored treasures in a place where force could rob them; I stored treasures where no force can harm them. They stored treasures that can yield no fruit; my treasures will be productive. They stored treasures of gold; I stored mine of souls. They stored treasures for others, I for my own good. They stored up treasures for this world, but I have stored mine for the World to Come." [Tosefta, Peah 4:18]

In Pirke Avot we read,

The work of righteousness

בִּשְׁעַת פְּטִירָתוֹ שֶׁל אָדָם. אֵין מְלַוִּים לוֹ לְאָדָם לֹא כֶסֶף.
וְלֹא זָהָב. וְלֹא אֲבָנִים טוֹבוֹת וּמַרְגָּלִיּוֹת. אֶלָּא תוֹרָה
וּמַעֲשִׂים טוֹבִים בִּלְבָד.

In the hour of man's death, neither silver nor gold nor precious stones nor pearls go with him, but only Torah and good works . . . [Avot 6:9]

What are we making ourselves worth? What values do we accept for ourselves? At the end of our lives, what remains with us is only "Torah and good works."

Your worth revolves around what you *make* yourself worth; your value depends on the values you allow to rule your actions.

The Ḥassidim loved to tell and retell the story of Reb Zusya of Hanipol, who taught his greatest lesson as he lay dying:

The students of Reb Zusya, hearing that their teacher was about to die, came to pay him one last visit. But entering the room, they were surprised to see him trembling with fear.

"Why are you afraid of death?" they asked. "In your life, have you not been as righteous as Moses himself?"

"When I stand before the throne of judgment," Zusya answered, "I will not be asked, 'Reb Zusya, why were you not like Moses?' I will be asked, 'Reb Zusya, why were you not like Zusya?'"

Reflection Clearly, each of us must strive to weave the cloth of righteousness in the loom of our lives, in the unique way that makes us each special beings apart from all others, in the way that gives to each of our lives a meaning far greater than the meaning of possessions and riches. This way of measuring the worth of your life is a part of your Jewish tradition, a part of the values that the Jewish people holds.

Each of us must strive to be the best "me" possible. That is the way a Jew measures the worth of his life.

6

The value of awareness

Inside each human being there is a sense that is as basic to us as our senses of sight, sound, touch, taste, and smell. And like these other senses, this inner sense can be developed and strengthened with exercise and use.

This inner sense is our religious awareness. It is our ability to discover what is sacred in the world around us. It is our ability to see what is possible in what already exists, our ability to sense the right action to take even when we cannot find a law or mitzvah that decides for us.

Perhaps the simplest way to understand how our religious awareness works is to use a concrete example. The same Reb Zusya of Hanipol of whom we spoke in the last chapter was stricken with blindness toward the end of his life.

Religious awareness and Zusya

Now, whenever tragedy strikes us or a person whom we hold dear, and even when it just comes near us, we begin to lean naturally to the side of our Yetzer HaRa. The Yetzer probes us, asking, "Would God let this happen? How can a person suffer so much? Why does God not put an end to suffering?"

Overcoming tragedy takes great strength, but it also requires us to use our sense of religious awareness. Reb Zusya assigned himself the difficult task of finding a blessing where there seemed to be only a curse. Using his religious awareness to overcome the force of Yetzer HaRa within him, he offered up this prayer: "Thank you, O Lord, for making me blind so that I might see the inner light."

There is no law commanding us to thank God for making us blind. It would be a cruel and bitter law. And there is no commandment that requires us to accept whatever happens without ever being angry, disappointed, or discouraged. But the religious awareness within us helps us to see that, because life is sacred, we must keep our balance between the Yetzer Tov and the Yetzer HaRa, we must never stop living and trusting.

What Reb Zusya found through his religious awareness, or religious imagination, is that no blindness could be so destructive as the blindness of the heart.

Using religious awareness   Like any of our senses, the inner sense of religious awareness must be used constantly if it is to serve us in times of need. The story is told of a farmer who stood at the fence bordering his field every day at the same hour to see the prince ride by on his white charger. One day the farmer noticed that it was not the prince riding the beautiful horse, but one of the prince's stable hands. "Hey!" the farmer called, "does the prince actually allow you to ride his own white horse?"

"Fool!" the servant replied, "when the prince is away, the horse must still be exercised."

What is true of the white charger is true of our religious awareness, too. Even where there is no urgent need for this special sense, it must still be exercised if it is to be kept in tiptop condition.

The rabbis realized this need and helped develop ways of making our religious awareness more sensitive. To do this, they designated special times for us to set aside in order to search for the sacred within the ordinary.

An obvious example of this is the ceremony of Bar Mitzvah or Bat Mitzvah. Almost all cultures and religions have some sort of ceremony to mark the time in a young person's life when he or she begins to take on personal responsibility with the group. Usually we call this point a "coming of age"—and our ceremony is certainly that. But how does Bar or Bat Mitzvah cause you to use your religious awareness?

Awareness in time and space

The ceremony itself is one answer. Each person senses a very special kind of attention that is his or hers alone on the day of Bar or Bat Mitzvah. It is the attention of the group, the feeling gained through publicly receiving the responsibility for the mitzvot.

The holidays are times when our religious awareness is exercised, too. On Passover, for example, we are commanded to say, "We celebrate because of what the Lord did for me when I came forth out of Egypt" (referring to Exod. 13:8). Ordinarily we think of ourselves as we see ourselves—in this place and in this time, at present. But here the Bible is asking us to see ourselves *before we were born*—as a part of something that happened thousands of years ago. At first it seems strange, but the more we begin to think about it, the more realistic it truly is. Our religious awareness is a part of our heritage as a people, and our heritage as a people certainly takes us back to the time of Egyptian slavery—and even before then. Passover gives us a chance to use our religious awareness in discovering a sacred way of understanding time.

Most brilliant example of them all, the Sabbath shines. Once a week, we Jews set apart a space in time and make it holy. Without the Sabbath, we tend to get caught up forever in everyday matters: day passes into day without end.

Setting apart the Sabbath for the purpose of resting our bodies provides a sacred time during which our religious awareness can be exercised like the prince's charger. We can see how the past week went for us and consider what the week to come will be like. We can find what is good and useful in what we do, and think of how we may improve upon it. We can sort out those things that are not worthwhile and find ways to change.

SEARCHING FOR THE SACRED

Our religious awareness needs to be exercised like the prince's white charger. Special occasions like Bar or Bat Mitzvah, Passover, and our weekly Shabbat remind us to stop and search for "the sacred within the ordinary."

Most of all, the Sabbath provides us with a foretaste of the World to Come. On the Sabbath we use our religious awareness to try to create a certain comfortable physical feeling around us, a sensation of the world at peace and at rest.

Our religious awareness or sensibility is sparked by prayer, too. Prayer is the way in which we express our emotions about the world around us. Beauty, agony, love, despair, want, and fear are all expressed through prayer and the ritual of the prayer service. The rabbis created an exercise for the religious awareness in their quest to find enough reasons to say 100 berachot every day.

Prayer and religious awareness

Searching for opportunities to pray throughout the day makes us constantly aware of the sacred and holy nature of life itself. Each berachah helps to remind us of God's place in the world. As God said to Moses, "All my goodness shall pass before you" [Exod. 33:19].

Knowing how easily we tend to get caught up in the ordinary, everyday things in our lives, the rabbis set aside special times for prayers. Morning, noon, and night these times present us with the opportunities to set our goals a little higher, with chances to use our religious awareness.

But special times and other opportunities for prayer are of little use unless we use our religious awareness in our actions as well. Based on the commandments of the Torah, we have constructed a way of life that turns upon itself—a way of life in which every religious action stirs the religious awareness to another religious action. One good deed draws another in its wake.

Awareness in our deeds

As Jews we believe that there is a purpose in God's creation and that each of us has a part in the working out of that purpose. How can we tell today, the rabbis asked, how important we may become tomorrow?

No man has the right to injure himself, to ruin himself, to murder himself. Everyone bears the duty to preserve himself physically. He may not weaken himself, for he knows not how his world will stand in need of him. [*Horeb,* Samuel Raphael Hirsch]

In addition, we bear the duty of holding our religious awareness ready so that we may discover what the Lord requires of us.

Awareness and vision The greatest instances of the use of religious awareness were provided by the Prophets of biblical times. Isaiah, for example, lived in a prosperous time. All around him people were successful and happy. It was a time of peace between nations, for the most part. Yet Isaiah issued a stern prophetic warning. For he saw that in the midst of plenty there was poverty; that while some waxed ever richer, others became poorer and poorer. This is not the Jewish dream, he taught: the Jewish dream is of a different kind of richness and a different kind of peace.

"To what purpose," Isaiah asked his generation, "is the multitude of your sacrifices unto [the Lord]?" [Isa. 1:11]. The sacrifices in the Temple cannot make up for the injustices that a person does in his everyday actions.

Saith the Lord:
I . . . delight not in the blood of bullocks, or of lambs. . . .
Put away the evil of your doings from before Mine eyes:
Cease to do evil;
Learn to do well;
Seek justice, relieve the oppressed. . . .
Come now, and let us reason together,
saith the Lord. [Isa. 1:11–18]

Isaiah's religious awareness foretold of a future in which

the wolf shall dwell with the lamb,
and the leopard lie down with the kid. [Isa. 11:6]

For out of Zion shall go forth the law,
And the word of the Lord from Jerusalem.
And they shall beat their swords into plowshares,
And their spears into pruning-hooks;
Nation shall not lift up sword against nation,
Neither shall they learn war any more. [Isa. 2:3–4]

Isaiah directed his religious awareness not to some other world or some time after death, but to this world and to the way things could be if we worked at them. God will not change our swords into plowshares: we must beat them ourselves if we wish them to be changed. If we desire the end to all wars, we must cease the "learning" of war. If we wish to see poverty and hunger removed from our community, we must "seek justice" and "relieve the oppressed."

Religious awareness, then, also helps us to overcome our apathy. Human beings have a tendency to say, "The work is too great for me alone, so I will not even try to do it." Our religious awareness helps us overcome that tendency. It helps us stand up to be counted, to say, "I can help—even if only a little." You might ask yourself a question that is only too familiar, "If I do not do my part, who will do it for me?"

Utopia

Many people have dreamed of "utopias"—societies that are perfect in every way. Some have even tried to create utopias by forming small communities built upon very strict rules that every member must follow. Few of these communities have succeeded. Even the most successful of them would not suit the temperament and character of all people, and in that sense they are not really perfect.

We have a vision of what life on earth can be—a
vision given us by the Prophets. Our religious
awareness helps keep that vision shining. Thus we
press on toward the goal of freedom, peace, and
plenty for all.

   The rabbis realized that it is not the structure of society at
fault when an attempted utopia fails, it is the *members* of
the society who cause it (or allow it) to fail. Even our own
society could approach perfection if every member came
closer to living in the image of God. The rabbis taught that
each of us must work at becoming a utopia in miniature, a
perfect society of one. In that way, our whole society would
be bettered.
   This, too, was the vision of the Prophets, the vision
underlying all religious awareness. Such vision involves
the ability to foresee what could be a better future and what
is presently a better direction.

Now you can understand how Zusya's reaction to becoming blind is such a good example of how we use our religious awareness. Zusya was setting a direction for a better future. Allowing the Yetzer HaRa to take over would have meant for Zusya a bitter present and a bleak tomorrow. Complaining and wallowing in misery would have destroyed all of Zusya's previous life work by giving his students and neighbors good reason to question his sincerity—even though some complaining and bitterness are only human and normal. In finding a blessing even in tragedy, Zusya rose above the normal and came closer to the image of God in which we are all created. Through his religious awareness, Zusya established a new future for himself.

The kinds of flowers we can expect to enjoy in the future always depend on the kinds of seeds we are willing to plant today. But planting for the future requires awareness, foresight, and imagination—the ability to see what is possible and to direct our actions according to what is best.

The Prophets had just such foresight and helped our people to visualize a future toward which to aim. Their visions have become our goals and continue to help us better understand our own religious imagination.

But if our religious imagination is to be of any use to us, we must exercise it every day in the same way as the prince's horse had to be exercised in order to stay fit for the prince's use. When our religious awareness is adequately prepared, it can help us overcome even deep personal tragedy and serve us as a guide in using our Yetzer HaRa in constructive instead of destructive ways.

When we use our religious awareness to guide us in our actions, we are planting the seeds of a better future for ourselves and, through us, for our community as well. As Ben Hai Hai said:

לְפֻם צַעֲרָא אַגְרָא:

According to the work is the reward. [Avot 5:26]

7

The value of knowledge

Our religious awareness alone is not enough to guide our actions. People sometimes get carried away by their religious feelings. You may have even heard people say at one time or another that there should be no such thing as religion: religion, they say, causes wars.

In truth, it is people who cause wars. But people have used religion as an excuse for war, time and time again. In a religious war, both sides can truly believe that God is with them alone, not with the enemy. Yet it is obvious to anyone who studies history that it could not possibly be so.

God is actually with both sides—only both sides have forgotten God and His commandments. Both sides have forgotten the true meaning of God and believe that they are doing what is good, when actually they are destroying what is good. It is a case of runaway religious awareness.

Gathering evidence   To avoid falling into this trap, we must learn to gather evidence carefully before we take serious action. Not only must we make our choices in the light of our religious awareness, but we should also try to make them intelligent ones. In the history of religions, three major ways of gathering evidence for choice-making have been tried. The earliest (and one that is still practiced today) is superstition. The second method is a system of fixed ethics. And the third way is the process of study.

Superstition has probably proved to be the most destructive method of gathering evidence. This is because superstition is so often the result of confused thinking. It usually starts out as something sensible: for example, a rule is made that a person near a construction site should not walk under a ladder when someone is on the ladder laying bricks. Why? Because he might just get struck on the head by a falling brick! That's not a bad rule for construction sites. It's not even a bad rule in general. Whenever someone is working above you on a ladder, it is best to avoid walking under it.

Superstition

But it is silly to believe that the simple *act* of walking under a ladder will bring you bad luck.

Of course, this is a fairly harmless example of how superstition arises. Superstition can grow very powerful, ugly, and mean. For hundreds of years, for example, the Catholic Church warned people to beware of Jews around Passover time. They claimed that Jews would steal Christian children, sacrifice them, and use their blood to bake *matzah*. You might think that only primitive people could believe such a tale, but even in our own century a Jewish man in Russia was charged with "blood libel" and tried for this alleged crime. In fact, each of the jurors swore that, apart from this particular case, he *believed* that Jews actually do this.

In this case, letters of protest were written by intelligent men and women worldwide, all enraged that such a superstition left over from the Dark Ages could still be considered "fact" in modern times. Finally the accused Jew was found innocent—not because the jury failed to accept the idea of "blood libel," but because there was no real evidence at all.

We like to feel that we know how things come about in the world. We like to link outcomes or effects to causes. But when we don't really have enough facts— or when we don't bother to think quite straight with those we do have—we may come up with a false "connection" between events. That is how superstitions arise.

How does superstition work as a means of gathering evidence? It claims to work very "scientifically." But superstition often connects an effect with the wrong cause.

Let's say that you had never seen a school before and that one day you are standing on a corner outside a large school building observing what is going on. In the morning, people gather outside, a bell rings, the people move inside the school and settle down. A while later the bell rings again, people begin moving around again, and once more they settle down. All day long, whenever the bell rings, people move around and then settle down. At the end of the day, the bell rings and the people leave. Now, if you were superstitious, you might very well conclude that the bell literally causes the people to move! You might say: the god of the bell controls the actions of the people, and "school" is a place where people worship a bell by moving at its command.

Superstition has given rise to some very ugly beliefs, as well as some very beautiful ones. The beautiful ones we call *myths,* and some myths are very moving stories that contain very real human truths. Other myths, not so glorious, reflect and bring about persecution and prejudice. Blood libels and witch-hunts show why we should not rely upon superstition as a basis for deciding how to act.

Fixed Ethics A much better system of gathering evidence relies on fixed ethics, laws that are for the most part unchanging or very difficult to change. A person who lives by a fixed ethic memorizes it and follows it day by day, perhaps unthinkingly.

A good system of fixed ethics is the law of the United States. Ancient Roman law also was a system of fixed ethics. Among religions and philosophies, the most famous system of fixed ethics is that of the great Chinese philosopher and teacher Confucius (551–479 B.C.E.). Here are a few of the ethical principles recorded in Confucius' masterwork, the Analects:

The Master said, "Work on strange doctrines does harm." [Analects 3:16]

The Master said, "A gentle person considers what is right; the vulgar considers what will pay." [Analects 4:16]

Meng Yi asked the duty of a son.
The Master said: "Obedience."
As Fan Ch'ih was driving him, the Master said: "Meng [Yi] asked me the duty of a son; I answered 'Obedience.'"
"What did ye mean?" said Fan Ch'ih.
"To serve our parents whilst they live," said the Master; "to bury them with all courtesy when they die; and to worship them with all courtesy." [Analects 3:5]

The Master angled, but did not fish with a net; he shot, but not at birds sitting. [Analects 7:26]

The Master said: "Study as though the time were short, as one who fears to lose." [Analects 8:17]

Confucius said: "The best people are born wise. Next come those who grow wise by learning: then, learned, narrow minds. Narrow minds, without learning, are the lowest of the people." [Analects 16:9]

You can see that some of Confucius' thoughts closely resemble some that we can find in Judaism. Although we do not worship our ancestors as Confucius taught, we do honor them; and honoring our parents is one of the Ten Commandments.

A system of fixed ethics such as Roman Law or the principles of Confucius can be good. It can also become evil, for it does not allow for the person with a questioning mind. It does not allow for openness and change. It allows no room for doubt. And it may easily lead to the habit of blindly following a leader and obeying authority without thinking.

Such was the case with Hitler and Nazi Germany, where the entire system of both Jewish and Christian ethics were overthrown and the evil value system of "might makes right" was officially established in its place.

After the war, countless German soldiers and workers blandly professed that they had only been "following orders" when they committed crimes against their neighbors. Had they been trained to think and choose with open minds, they would have found it difficult to fall into this trap of blind obedience.

Judaism and ethics Fixed ethics and superstition are not necessarily evil in themselves, but they give way easily to force. The problem with these two systems of gathering evidence is the same: they do not require the learner to keep an open mind. Superstition rests on fear, and fixed ethics often rely much too heavily on prejudice—that is to say, judging before all the facts are in.

Judaism uses all three methods of gathering evidence —the two already discussed, as well as study—in order to form judgments. Naturally, superstition is the one used least often. It is the least reliable and the one most easily mistaken. Here is an example of superstitious fact-gathering from Pirke Avot:

> *At four periods disease increases: in the fourth year, in the seventh, at the conclusion of the seventh year, and at the end of the Feast of Tabernacles each year. In the fourth year, because some did not give the proper amount of charity to the poor in the third year. In the seventh year, because some did not give the proper amount of charity to the poor in the sixth year. At the conclusion of the seventh year, because some do not observe the laws regarding the fruits of the seventh year. And at the end of the Feast of Tabernacles each year, because some rob the poor of the portions legally assigned to them. [Avot 5:12]*

We may smile in amusement at this belief that harming the poor brings evil and disease upon the community as a whole, and we may believe that God would not be so cruel as to make the innocent suffer along with the guilty. Yet, in a way, we can understand the reasoning behind it, just as we understand the point when a teacher punishes an entire class—say, by keeping them ten minutes after school—because one or two of the class members were disrupting the lesson. In a way, the whole class *is* responsible. Using the same sort of reasoning, the rabbis believed that God holds the whole community responsible for those who do not bear a fair share of the burden of helping the poor.

Still, superstition such as this is not so reliable as beliefs based on actual data. It can get in the way of making truly intelligent decisions in regard to important problems. So Judaism no longer relies on superstition to any significant degree.

Nor do we rely on fixed ethics to guide us. As Jews we place great value on the religious awareness of each person while still believing that one set of ethics can be right for all people. So we do have a system of fixed ethics that provides guidelines.

Judaism and fixed ethics

The most famous of these ethics is the Decalogue, the Ten Commandments, which are so universally accepted that they have become the basis for all truly ethical systems of law in the Western World. Each of these commandments is supported by whole systems of Jewish values, too.

CONSIDERING THE CIRCUMSTANCES

The Ten Commandments provide firm guidelines for conduct. But even the absolute commandment against murder may be set aside in a case of self-defense. In judging, Jews always ask, "What were the circumstances?"

For example, "Thou shalt not murder," is a command-ment that contains in its brief and urgent message worlds of Jewish thought and belief. In it is the Jewish idea that each of us is more than clay and dust; that each person is holy and sacred. Underlying this commandment is the Jewish value that holds that life itself is sacred, that no life is created by accident. The commandment not to murder says in effect that destruction of the community results from killing just one of its members. It reminds us that each person is unique, a world unto himself. "Thou shalt not murder" can be considered a fixed ethic: a person is not even allowed to murder someone who has committed murder.

A Sanhedrin [court] which executed a person once in seven years was called destructive. Rabbi Eleazar ben Azariah said, Once in seventy years. Rabbi Tarphon and Rabbi Akiba said, If we were members of a Sanhedrin, never would a person be put to death. [Mak. 1:10]

Only if the person standing before you is about to kill you are you allowed to murder, and then you must be sure that it is the intention of that person to murder you. Once you are sure, and see that there is no other way out, you must strike first!

The commandment "Thou shalt not murder" is one of three that are considered absolute and unchangeable, the other two being the ones forbidding adultery and idolatry. These might be considered "fixed ethics" in Judaism. Yet, as we have just noted, there is even one circumstance in which killing another person is permitted. So that you can see that Judaism does not rely solely or even primarily on fixed ethics, either.

Judaism and study   The rabbis presented a third alternative, which they con-sidered to include all three methods: study.

בֶּן־זוֹמָא אוֹמֵר. אֵיזֶהוּ חָכָם הַלּוֹמֵד מִכָּל אָדָם. שֶׁנֶּאֱמַר
מִכָּל מְלַמְּדַי הִשְׂכַּלְתִּי.

Ben Zoma said, "Who is wise? He who learns from all men; as it is said, From all my teachers I have gotten understanding." [Avot 4:1]

"Learning from all" is a Jewish value. The rabbis often told stories of how simple folk taught wise lessons in behavior.

Rabbi Joshua was once walking by the way when he saw a shortcut through a field where a small path had been beaten by other travelers. He began to make his way across the field, but in the center he met a girl.
"Where do you think you are going?" she asked.
"I am walking across this field to the other side," he replied.
"This is my father's field," she said to him.
"I am only following a path which is already made," the rabbi said.
"Yes," the girl said. "But the path was made by others like you who have already harmed the crops. Will you follow in their footsteps to do evil?" [Erub. 53b]

It is amazing not only that the girl taught Rabbi Joshua ben Hananiah a lesson, but that the story was recorded and passed on to us! In other words, the rabbis wanted us to study it in order to see two things: (1) that a person should not follow others to do evil, and (2) that a person (even the wisest rabbi) can learn from anyone.

The aim of Jewish study, of course, is practice—in the art of choosing Jewishly.

הַלּוֹמֵד עַל מְנָת לְלַמֵּד. מַסְפִּיקִים בְּיָדוֹ לִלְמֹד וּלְלַמֵּד.
וְהַלּוֹמֵד עַל מְנָת לַעֲשׂוֹת. מַסְפִּיקִים בְּיָדוֹ לִלְמֹד וּלְלַמֵּד
לִשְׁמֹר וְלַעֲשׂוֹת:

Rabbi Ishmael . . . said, He who learns in order to teach, Heaven will grant him the opportunity both to learn and to teach; but he who learns in order to act, Heaven will grant him the opportunity to learn and to teach, to observe and to act. [Avot 4:6]

You could argue that just because Judaism teaches that we *should* study does not mean that we *must* study. That is

Having a preference

true. On the other hand, a part of making choices is having a preference.

You may have a favorite color, a favorite flavor of ice cream, a favorite day of the week, a favorite teacher, and so on. Such preferences help you when you make decisions. Much of the problem of everyday choices is solved when you already have preferences.

As Jews, our people has traditionally and consistently expressed a preference for study. (A concrete and living example of how this preference works is the fact that you now attend a Jewish school and study there. Whether you personally wanted to study there or are there only because your parents have chosen to send you, your presence there expresses a preference of knowledge over ignorance.)

It is easy to see how study helps us gather all the evidence and eliminate superstition and prejudice. Perhaps it is more difficult to understand that study can also help us to eliminate fear.

For us as Jews, study is like a key to the universe and its pleasures. Try to remember the worlds that opened to you as you learned how to read and write. Letters keep you in touch with people far away. Reading brings you worlds you have never seen. The imagination of a hundred writers meets your imagination, saddening you or amusing you, making you rejoice or forcing you to think deeply.

THREE-WAY BLESSING

Study can help dispel false fears. (Columbus's sailors were afraid they might sail off the edge of the earth, but Columbus was not.) Study can dispel false confidence, too. (If there is a real danger, you want to know about it, don't you?) And study can be a key to delights!

The rabbis described their preference for study in the strongest possible terms. They wanted their students to see how important study is to living a good life. For the rabbis, study provided opportunities for unraveling the great mysteries of creation. And thus study was made the duty of each and every Jew.

Rabbi Jonah said:

> He who has not studied at all is like a beast, for he was created solely for the purpose of learning and studying the Torah, whose ways are ways of pleasantness.
>
> Now, if a person has not studied at all and if he persists in such wickedness, he does not deserve to live even one day, even one hour. [Commentary]

A person has no excuse, the rabbis instructed us—you must study. Whether you are rich or poor, young or old.

No excuse

> A poor man and a rich one died at about the same time and presented themselves to the heavenly court. The poor man was asked: "Why did you not spend more time studying?" He answered, "I was poverty-stricken and worried that I would not earn enough even to sustain my body." Then the court pointed to Hillel.
>
> For his daily work, Hillel earned only half a Roman denarius; still he supported himself on only a half of that and gave the other half to the keeper of the gate at the House of Study. After paying his admission fee, he would go into the House of Study and listen to the words of the sages Shemayah and Avtalion.
>
> One day, he could find no work at all; and the doorkeeper refused to admit him to the House of Study unless he could pay the fee. So Hillel climbed up on the roof and sat outside the skylight window in order to hear the day's lesson.
>
> Now it happened that this was in midwinter on the eve of Sabbath, and snow fell heavily. The next morning, Shemayah said to Avtalion, "My colleague, usually the room is light, but today it is dark; perhaps it is cloudy?" But looking up they saw the form of a man on the skylight.
>
> Immediately they went out and discovered Hillel on the rooftop, frozen almost to death. They rubbed and dried him and built a fire in the fireplace, saying, "This man is deserving to have the Sabbath broken in order to save his life."

Tradition tells us that Hillel was admitted without charge after that to the House of Study. [Yoma 35b]

But what about the rich man?

The rich man was asked, "Why did you not spend more time studying?" He answered, "I was worried about all my possessions and property and I spent my time taking care of it all."

Then the court said, "Were you more wealthy than Eleazar, whose father promised him a thousand cities and a fleet of a thousand ships?" Still every day he slung a bag of flour over his shoulder and went from city to city and from province to province to study Torah. Using the flour as payment for his lessons, he learned from whoever would teach him. [Yoma 35b]

Rich or poor, every Jew is required to study. Young and old alike must study, too.

Rabbi Akiba says: If you have studied Torah in your youth, study Torah in your old age. Say not, "I shall not study Torah in my old

age," for you do not know whether you will understand better young or old. [ARN 3]

Akiba himself did not begin to study the Torah until he was forty years old!

Reflection

Religious awareness alone is not enough. Though it shows us the world the way we would like it to be, it does not give us the answers to the immediate problems we face. These answers require the gathering of evidence.

In the history of religions, three main systems have been used for finding and collecting the facts we need in order to make intelligent decisions on how to act. Superstition, the first system, relies too heavily on fear and has the ugly ability to allow people to believe in a lie long after it has been proved false.

The second system, that of fixed ethics, is somewhat better. It is often used for the good of its followers, but it can be harmful when carried to an extreme because it does not require the individual to think for himself, to think openly and honestly, and to doubt.

The third system is study. Judaism uses all three systems. Our preference is for study. Whether a Jew is young or old, rich or poor, study opens the mind and allows him to choose freely. Study is an excellent means of gathering the evidence we need, of finding the right amount of fixed ethics to follow, and of sorting out truth from superstition.

Your own study helps you to grow and develop in positive ways. It helps you to make choices that will benefit your world and the worlds of all the people you contact. Especially as you choose the kind of career you wish to pursue, the kinds of friends you wish to make, the kind of community in which you wish to live, and the kind of world you want for your children and for your children's children, study can help you to make intelligent decisions.

Together, study and religious awareness will help you to find what kind of a person you might be and how you might benefit all humanity. Only through study can a person learn what it means to grow in the image of God.

8

The value of study

You spend a great deal of time studying. You study in your schoolwork. You study in your Jewish school. You may also study piano, guitar, or some other musical instrument. You may have studied dancing, drama, fencing, writing, art, knitting, or karate. Probably you have spent some time studying hobbies and learning the rules to dozens of games. So much of your life depends on study!

The rabbis believed that study is an important path to action. In a way, all of your studies result in actions. We could even say that study itself is a kind of action. As you study, you find out what is truly important, and that helps you make intelligent choices about what you want to do.

Rabbi Meir encouraged his students to spend less time working at growing rich and more time in studying Torah:

הֱוֵי מְמַעֵט בְּעֵסֶק וַעֲסֹק בַּתּוֹרָה. וֶהֱוֵי שְׁפַל רוּחַ בִּפְנֵי כָל אָדָם. וְאִם בָּטַלְתָּ מִן הַתּוֹרָה. יֶשׁ־לְךָ בְּטֵלִים הַרְבֵּה כְּנֶגְדֶּךָ. וְאִם עָמַלְתָּ בַתּוֹרָה. יֶשׁ־לוֹ שָׂכָר הַרְבֵּה לִתֶּן־לָךְ:

Lessen your toil for worldly goods, and be busy in the Torah. . . . If you neglect the Torah, many causes for neglecting it will you find, but if you labor in the Torah, God will find many ways of rewarding you. [Avot 4:12]

The rabbis believed worldly riches to be only a temporary kind of achievement. A person who has become rich may all too easily feel that all is won. But the truth of the matter is that the riches of the world always remain in the world. They never really belong to anyone except for a short period of time. But studies are gained for ever. What you learn cannot be stolen from you, and you can lose it only if you neglect it.

Nevertheless, study is work. As Rabbi Meir said, you must "labor in the Torah." You already know how much work study can be. It may mean memorizing or practicing a lesson over and over. You may have to prepare for examinations. You may have to write papers or book reports. It may mean reading, rereading, and remembering. You may have to fight to understand the lesson.

Study is work

And just as in other kinds of work, there is no guarantee that you will succeed. Some studies may be easy for you and others just too difficult. You may find that sometimes you just want to throw up your hands in despair and say, "Why should I bother? I'm not really getting anywhere."

THE WINNERS!

**Only one person may win the race.
How many gain
from the running?**

Study is its own reward There is an answer. Success is not the only reward. No matter what the task, and regardless of whether you succeed in it, the real reward is in the doing. In a very special sense, then, study is its own reward.

> *Rabbi Meir said, Whoever labors in the Torah for its own sake [that is, without thought of success], serves many things; and not only so, but the whole world is in debt to him: he is called friend, beloved, a lover of the All-present, a lover of mankind: it clothes him in meekness and reverence; it fits him to become just, pious, upright, and faithful; it keeps him far from sin, and brings him near to virtue: through him the world enjoys counsel and sound knowledge. [Avot 6:1]*

Especially in the task of preparing youself for action, the rabbis taught, your attitude should be that the truest rewards are always in the doing. Take the case of being a student. We do not all have the same qualities as students, we are not all equally equipped for each area of study. Some of us are better at some studies than at others. But our attitude should be that all studies are worthwhile because *studying* is worthwhile.

Four qualities The rabbis, who spent much of their time studying and teaching, found that there are four different qualities or approaches that a person can bring to study. These are the four extremes among students. Actually, the rabbis realized that most of us do not tend to be so extreme. But knowing the four extremes can help you decide the direction in which you would like to change your own ap-

CHANGING OUR ATTITUDES

We cannot change our attitudes as readily as we change our clothes. But we can, with a little reflection, check them, and see if they fit the learning task at hand.

proach. See which of these descriptions is most like you; and then see which of them you most wish to be like.

The first extreme among students is the one who is

The first quality

מָהִיר לִשְׁמֹעַ וּמָהִיר לְאַבֵּד. יָצָא שְׂכָרוֹ בְּהֶפְסֵדוֹ.

quick to understand and quick to forget—his gain is canceled by his loss. [Avot 5:15]

If you are like this student, you gain an understanding of the lesson rapidly while you study it, but lose it just as rapidly afterward. This student fails really to profit by study. For this problem, the rabbis offered a simple and sure remedy: as soon as you understand the lesson, repeat it; then repeat it again and again until you are sure that it is fixed in your memory.

Repetition is also a good technique for the student who is at the second extreme, who is

The second quality

קָשֶׁה לִשְׁמֹעַ וְקָשֶׁה לְאַבֵּד. יָצָא הֶפְסֵדוֹ בִּשְׂכָרוֹ.

slow to understand and slow to forget—his loss is cancelled by his gain. [Avot 5:15]

If you are like this student, learning seems a difficult task indeed. But it can be a great triumph, too. For once you have learned a thing, you do not easily forget it.

Rabbi Nathan, in his commentary on Pirke Avot, calls the third kind of student a "winner." This is the student who succeeds easily in studies, who is

The third quality

מָהִיר לִשְׁמֹעַ וְקָשֶׁה לְאַבֵּד. זֶה חֵלֶק טוֹב.

quick to understand and slow to forget—this is a happy fortune. [Avot 5:15]

If you are this kind of student, you are lucky indeed. But

even then you must work at studying, for the moment you stop studying, your learning ceases. This third kind of student, for whom study comes so easily, must still *remember to study!*

The fourth quality

There is a fourth extreme among students—the student who is

קָשֶׁה לִשְׁמֹעַ וּמָהִיר לְאַבֵּד. זֶה חֵלֶק רָע.

slow to understand and quick to forget—this is an unfortunate lot. [*Avot 5:15*]

Yet the rabbis saw hope for even this unfortunate, who can neither understand easily nor remember long. And that is why we have spoken of four qualities. The rabbis believed, not that people are born knowing how to study, but that we *learn* how to study. That is why your attitude toward study is so important. It may even affect the *quality* of your study. When you study with a positive attitude, your study carries its own blessing.

Even the unfortunate fourth extreme of student receives the reward of playing the game by continuing to study. Of course, when you experience difficulties like those of the fourth kind of student, the Yetzer HaRa steps in, too. You might come to feel that getting a good grade is more important than studying. Why not cheat?

Winning and losing

If you were playing tennis with a friend and every time you served the ball your friend caught it and ran to the net, yelling, "Touchdown!" you might get very tired of playing tennis. If you were playing volleyball and the other team began to run under the net and play on both sides of the court, you would tell them that it is against the rules.

They might answer, "We'll play by the rules as long as we are winning. When we are losing, we'll cheat." Then you would probably reply, "That's childish!"

It is equally childish to imagine that cheating at study means winning. The person who cheats loses entirely. Not only does the cheater fail to learn the lesson, but he does not really gain anything, either. A good grade is only a *sign* of achievement, it is not really the achievement itself. Cheating in order to receive a decent or high grade is like going down to a store and buying yourself a bowling trophy—it really never means much to you.

Yet this is a very complex subject. To be honest, we have to admit that in some ways grades do count. You are under a lot of pressure to get good grades; you are under a lot of pressure to be a good student. Sometimes these two are the same, and sometimes they are not. Sometimes it is just plain difficult to know what is really important.

But cheating only empties us of the real challenges of freedom. When we cheat we are not only stealing what properly belongs to someone else, we are stealing from our own spirit. Inside it makes us feel smaller. Facing the real challenges around us takes more courage and means accepting more responsibility for ourselves, but it safeguards our freedom and keeps us honest. When we face our problems openly and courageously, we suddenly see that cheating can never give us strength where we are weak.

When it comes to study, the answer lies in learning to use our memory in the best possible way. As a guide, the rabbis described four extremes of memory, each in terms of a word-picture:

What has value?

LEARNING TO LEARN

We must study how to study. A student, like an athlete, can face his weaknesses and learn to overcome them; can learn his strengths and make the most of them.

סְפוֹג. וּמַשְׁפֵּךְ. מְשַׁמֶּרֶת. וְנָפָה. סְפוֹג שֶׁהוּא סוֹפֵג אֶת־הַכֹּל. וּמַשְׁפֵּךְ שֶׁמַּכְנִיס בְּזוֹ וּמוֹצִיא בְּזוֹ. מְשַׁמֶּרֶת שֶׁמּוֹצִיאָה אֶת־הַיַּיִן וְקוֹלֶטֶת אֶת־הַשְּׁמָרִים. וְנָפָה שֶׁמּוֹצִיאָה אֶת־הַקֶּמַח וְקוֹלֶטֶת אֶת־הַסֹּלֶת:

a sponge, which soaks up everything; a funnel, which lets in at one end and out at the other; a strainer, which lets the wine pass through and retains the dregs; [and] a sieve, which lets out the coarse and retains the fine flour. [Avot 5:18]

At first you may think it best to have a memory like "a sponge, which soaks up everything." And surely, that is better than the "funnel, which lets in at one end and out at the other." It might also seem better to have a memory like "a sieve, which lets out the coarse and retains the fine flour," than like "a strainer, which lets the wine pass through and retains the dregs." But actually, each of these types of memory helps the community in a different way, and we are always enriched when our group is blessed with all four kinds of memory.

The sponge

The memory like a sponge is what we today call a "photographic memory." It remembers all. As with a storehouse, everything may be put into it. The only possible problem with having this kind of memory is that the person may not always know what is important and what is not. But if a question should arise to which no one else can remember the answer—if, for example, we want to know the value of a dinar or the year in which the First Temple was destroyed— the sponge memory often has the answer at his fingertips.

The funnel

It is harder to see why the "funnel" memory is important. We all know people like this, and often laughingly say of them that information "goes in one ear and out the other." Among those with funnel memory is the student who studies carefully for every test and then forgets what he has learned as soon as the test is over. But there is a value to this kind of memory, too. Just as a funnel is wider at one end than at the other in order to help us pour from a wider jar into a smaller one, this memory helps a person to digest a great amount of knowledge and simplify it.

Oftentimes a good reporter is one who can listen to everyone's version of an incident and then write a short report that tells everything in a few words. This is a good application for the funnel-type memory.

The "sieve" memory seems a good kind to have. In some ways it is like the "sponge" and in other ways like the "funnel." Like the sponge memory, it remembers well; and like the funnel memory, it takes in much and is able to reduce it to a small amount. But unlike the sponge, it separates what is not worthwhile, retaining only what is truly important. And unlike the funnel, which basically only repeats what it has heard, it speaks with a new voice, explaining as it teaches.

The sieve

Hillel is a good example of the sieve-type memory. In saying, "Love your neighbor as yourself: that is the whole Torah; the rest is commentary—now go and study," Hillel summed up a vast amount of learning and study in a useful and brilliant way. He was indeed like the sieve, which separates out the coarse grain, allowing the finest flour to gather.

It is hardest to see how the "strainer" memory can be of any value. At first glance, it seems merely a nuisance—for it remembers the least important parts of everything. Still, everything is of some importance, and the strainer very often passes on "the wine" (that is, the good teachings) without even knowing it!

The strainer

To the men whose teachings make up Pirke Avot, study —especially the study of Torah—was an important subject. Because they were basically teachers and students themselves, they understood the problems of learning and remembering. The Talmud records a debate that took place at Lydda in which the question was, "Which is greater, study or action?"

Reflection

Rabbi Tarphon said, "Doing is the greater thing."

Rabbi Akiba said, "Study is the greater."

The majority of the rabbis agreed with Akiba and declared, "Study is the more important of these two, because study leads to action" [Kid. 40b].

Because of this attitude, the rabbis placed a great deal of importance on the study of Torah. They knew that there were other fields of study. In Pirke Avot, they called these other fields the "desserts" of study, tasty treats that a person should save for the end of the meal when the more nourishing food of Torah has already been completed.

Rabbi Eleazar Hisma said, The laws . . . are ordinances of import; astronomy and geometry are the desserts of wisdom. [*Avot 3:23*]

LABOR IN THE TORAH

When your family plans a trip, you need roadmaps and guidebooks. You want to know the best route to travel, the sights to seek out, the road hazards to avoid. The Torah is our roadmap and guidebook to living. The study of Torah is the study of life itself.

The study of Torah is paramount. It is most important for it is the practical study that leads to right action. The Torah is described as "a tree of life to them who hold it fast; its ways are ways of pleasantness and all its paths are peace" [Prov. 3:17, 18].

The rabbis, of course, saw that students approach study with different dispositions. Some remembered longer than others, some learned more quickly than others. They saw, too, that people had different ways of remembering, different kinds of memory. But this was not their main concern.

The rabbis were not trying to make everyone a great student or a rabbi. They did not wish everyone's memory to be like Hillel's. Instead, they were interested in assuring each person of some study of the Torah, enough so that the student would see what actions are Jewish, what dreams are Jewish, and what ideas are Jewish. The real blessing of study, therefore, is the study itself—because study leads to action.

Therefore they said, "Students of the wise enlarge peace in the world" [Ber. 64a].

9

The value of courage

If we place together some of the values we have studied, they lead us to an interesting question. We are taught that each of us is created in the image of God; that within each of us a struggle is going on between our Yetzer HaRa, our impulse toward selfishness, and our Yetzer Tov, our impulse toward holiness; and that each of us is given free will. We have seen that Judaism helps us to develop a religious awareness and trains us to gather evidence through study. Why, then, are we not required to be perfect?

The Nazirite In biblical times, as in all times, there were those who wished to live in the pure light of the spirit—those who wished to overcome their creatureliness, the animal nature within themselves, in order to draw closer to God and God's image. These people were called Nazirites. They vowed not to drink wine, to avoid contact with any dead body, and not to cut their hair.

While the rabbis did not approve of the way of the Nazirites, this form of self-dedication to God must have existed even before the Torah was written, and it became popular thereafter from time to time.

When the Temple was destroyed, the number of [Nazirites] was increased who would neither drink wine nor eat any meat. Rabbi Joshua went to them and asked why. They said, "How can we eat flesh now that the Temple is destroyed? It was the Temple that made flesh holy through sacrifices to God. And how can we drink wine, seeing that wine was used as a part of the Temple ceremony?"

Rabbi Joshua replied, "In that case how can you eat bread, seeing that the Temple's meal offerings are no more?"

They said, "Perhaps we shall live on fruit."

Joshua replied, "In that case we cannot eat fruit, for the offerings of first fruit [on Shavuot] are no more."

They replied, "Perhaps we can manage on fruits that were not used in the Temple ritual."

Rabbi Joshua then said, "Still you may drink no water, for water was used as a part of the Temple service."

Then they were silent.

But Rabbi Joshua added, "Not to mourn at all is impossible for us [for the Temple is actually destroyed]; but to mourn overmuch is also not possible for us. No religious duty is placed upon a community which the majority of the community can not endure." [Baba B. 60b]

From the argument of Rabbi Joshua we can see that the rabbis were not in favor of the extreme vows of the Nazirites. To help the Nazirites achieve a balanced view of reality, the Torah had set boundaries for Nazirite vows.

For one, the time limit of the vow (unless the Nazirite said otherwise) was set at thirty days. At the end of thirty days (or at the end of a longer vow) the Nazirite had to come to the Temple bringing four sacrifices, including "one ewe lamb of the first year without blemish for a sin offering" [Num. 6:14]. At that time, in a special room in the Temple set aside for the purpose, the Nazirite cut his hair, which was the sign of one following a vow.

Why should a person who had vowed to be holy and to consecrate himself as a Nazirite have to bring a "sin offering"? What sin did the Nazirite commit through vowing to be "holy unto the Lord"? [Num. 6:8].

Rabbi Eleazar HaKappar Berebi said: Against what soul did the Nazirite sin? It can only mean that he denied himself the enjoyment of wine. Now, if a person who denies himself only the enjoyment of wine is a sinner, all the more so one who denies himself all the enjoyments of life. [Taanit 11a–b]

The Holy One is within you

The rabbis' argument went on to point out that a person should not deny himself the pleasures of the world, because within each of us is a spark of the divine. As it is written in Hosea, "The Holy One is in the midst of you" [Hos. 11:9]. So to deny ourselves pleasure is to deny pleasure to God as well.

There is another reason for avoiding the extreme of asking perfection of ourselves. In the biblical stories, the heroes of the Jewish people ring true to life because they are pictured as actual human beings. That is, each of them is shown not only doing good, but in the exceptions in their lives, the sins that they committed. We believe in the reality of Moses who spoke with God because we know that Moses was a true man, since he is shown to have sinned, as all men must sin. We believe in the truth of the story of King David, because we understand how a King can sin through misusing his power. The story of King David would be an empty one indeed if it were the story of a perfect person! But even our sins prove that we can be holy if we are courageous enough to come to grips with the world of reality.

Side-stepping reality

The real sin of the Nazirites was sidestepping reality, failing to come to grips with the real problems of their time. The rabbis even warned them against repeating the period of their vows over and over, because soon they became charity cases as a result of neglecting their businesses and their families. True courage, the rabbis pointed out, requires action in the everyday world and a balance between the everyday realities of living and the eternal realities of life.

Sidestepping reality by trying to live in some interior world only demonstrates that you are afraid of the real

NEGATIVE VIRTUE

It takes courage to live in the world. Did you notice the number of prohibitions in the Nazirites' approach? Would you judge the Nazirites in some degree to be cowards or "cop-outs"?—or perhaps what psychologists call "compulsive perfectionists"? How did the rabbis try to bring them to a more balanced view of life?

world and afraid of yourself. In contrast, the rabbis pointed to the Torah, which commands us to act in the world:

> This commandment which I command you this day, it is not too hard for you, neither is it far off. It is not in heaven, that you should say: "Who will go up for us to heaven and bring it to us, and make us to hear it, that we may do it?" Neither is it beyond the sea, that you should say; "Who shall go over the sea for us, and bring it to us, and make us hear it, that we may do it?"
> But the word is very close to you—in your mouth, and in your heart, that you may do it. [Deut. 30:11–15]

One of the easiest things to do is let other people decide things for us. The easiest way to form an opinion is to listen to a news commentator and think whatever he seems to think. It is much more difficult to think for yourself—it means using your awareness and your ability to gather your own evidence.

Avoiding personal responsibility

In the time of the rabbis, the easiest course for a person to follow was to be another person's slave. Slavery then was a common practice, especially as payment for debts. Jewish slaves served a term of six years and were released in the seventh year according to biblical law.

But if a slave demanded to continue in his slavery at the end of a six-year term, claiming that he loved his master and wished to follow his master's way of life instead of accepting responsibility for his own way of life, then the Torah prescribes the following ritual: the slave is to be taken to the doorway and a hole bored in his earlobe with a hammer and awl. He must then serve until the Jubilee Year (which came once every fifty years) as an *eved nirtzah*, a "servant with the bored earlobe."

This sounds strange to us today. Why would a person *want* to be a slave? But our question is really a modern one. Slavery in ancient Israel, especially for the Hebrew slave, was not an evil practice. For it was expected, the Talmud explains

> *that the master should not eat white bread and the slave coarse bread, that the master should not drink old wine and the slave new wine, that the master should not sleep on a feather mattress and the slave on one of straw.* [Kid. 20a]

In modern terms, if you were the master and you owned two television sets, one black-and-white and one color, the slave should be given the color set to watch and you should watch the black-and-white one. Hence the saying "Whoever acquires a Hebrew slave, acquires a master for himself" [Kid. 20a].

Discouraging the choice of slavery

The rabbis believed that a person should be responsible for himself, that each person has the duty to face up to reality. Choosing to remain a slave is not a way of facing up to this responsibility, it is a way of sidestepping it. An eved nirtzah was a person who lacked the courage to be himself, by himself.

But what is the meaning of the strange ritual of boring a person's earlobe? Is this not barbaric? Doesn't the Torah also command us not to mark our bodies in any way?

Rabbi Yohanan ben Zakkai explained the commandment by reminding us that when the mitzvah of freedom was given to us at Mount Sinai, it was the *ear* that was

HEAR, O ISRAEL

With their ears the Jews at Sinai heard the Law given through Moses. They were to obey and understand, they were to have the courage to make choices as free individuals. Slavery was discouraged by marking the ear of any Jew who freely chose to remain a slave.

responsible for hearing and remembering [Exempla 277].

The ritual of boring the earlobe, then, was intended to dicourage those who wished to avoid self-responsibility. It forced the slave to decide for all time whether or not to be marked as one who shirked this responsibility. (Just the thought of the pain involved in having an ear bored through with a hammer and awl may have discouraged some.) Slavery became a physical mark upon the eved nirtzah, just as it was already a mark on his spirit. By using a hammer and awl, the master conveyed the true sound of bondage to the slave—the sound of chains being forged, the ringing sound that meant the slavery of the soul. The pounding would long echo in the ears of the eved nirtzah, the man who chose to remain in slavery.

Winning freedom

We must guard our freedom not only by rejecting slavery and oppression, but through positive action, by taking on responsibility. We must come face to face with our lives. Mordecai Kaplan (b. 1881), the founder of Reconstructionist Judaism, has observed that "it is much harder to live a life of freedom and self-rule than to be ruled by others" [Basic Values in Jewish Religion]. This is also the lesson of Abraham, who left his own birthplace and the people he knew, the home of his parents, in order to become closer to God and free to be responsible for his own way of life.

Guarding freedom All around us is the marketplace and the values of the marketplace. These values are a part of television and radio, of motion pictures and advertising, of magazines, newspapers, and books. Sometimes they are a part of our feelings for neighbors and friends. Often they are a part of our organized groups. Marketplace values endanger us today. While we are not likely to become slaves to another person, we are very much prone to becoming slaves to the values of the modern marketplace.

The values of the marketplace We are all aware of these dangers. If you watch too much television, you begin to believe that the really important values of life are always being clean, always being happy, always laughing when the studio audience laughs, or canned laughter appears on the soundtrack, and always being entertained. You might begin to think that the truly important decisions concern where to go on a vacation, what records to listen to, which brand of furniture polish or laundry detergent to use, which bank to place your money in, and, most urgent of all, which channel to tune in. Some of us become so involved in these values of the marketplace that when a television program ends and we are faced with choosing among channels for the next program, we may not realize that there is always another possible choice —the choice of whether to turn off the television set altogether.

Television provides a good example for our discussion here because it is so widely accepted that in some homes a television set is constantly on for twelve hours or more a day.

Telephones are usually involved with the values of the marketplace. We are so accustomed to answering the telephone when it rings that we do it slavishly. A ringing telephone more or less commands us to answer—we may even run to do it. But consider how slavish we are: If you are at home having a very serious talk with your best friend and the telephone rings, you forget your best friend, you forget your very serious conversation, and, even if it is a total stranger calling to ask you to subscribe to a magazine, your friend has to wait until you finish talking on the telephone.

It may sound strange, but learning how *not* to answer a ringing telephone is one of the most difficult tasks in the modern world. The telephone has become so firmly established by modern values that it may actually be easier for an adult to stop smoking than for him to think twice before answering a ringing telephone. The Jew who strictly observes Shabbat, who refuses to answer the telephone for a whole day, actually learns each Shabbat a part of the true meaning of the Jewish value of freedom of choice through not answering. Try not answering the telephone on Shabbat for two or three weeks and you will see what a different attitude you will have with regard to the telephone. For a change (once you have overcome that nagging suspicion that every call is an emergency), the telephone will become your slave rather than you being a slave to it.

There are so many more examples of this kind that each of us could write an entire book on the subject. We almost take for granted the values of the marketplace because they so completely surround us. Yet we react to the values of the marketplace constantly. We buy the records our friends buy, wear the same kind of clothes our friends wear, style our hair the "in" way. We begin to date when our friends begin to date. We laugh when they laugh. We cry when we are supposed to cry. We think only when we are forced to think, and even then only for short periods of time because it is so hard—there is no one inside to tell us what to think.

It is hard, very hard, to come to grips with reality. It is hard to stop the world long enough to ask: "What am I being sold? What values am I following that I have not bothered to think about? How many opinions have I adopted just because they are popular? How many things do I do that I really don't like doing, but that I am willing to do because other people do them?"

Coming to grips with reality

Facing reality takes courage. Creating an inner balance

between the realities and possibilities of this world requires bravery and stoutheartedness. Your religious awareness can help you achieve a special attitude toward the world around you, an attitude of hope and doubt, of responsibility and freedom—but you must *choose* to achieve it. Through study you can gather the evidence that will help you see what is right to believe and what is merely a marketplace value—but you must *choose* to study.

Inner strength In truth, even if we do not want to face reality, reality faces us. For one thing, each of us must die. No one is exempt. No one can avoid dying. But the fact that we must die actually makes our life more precious. The fact that each of us must come to grips with the reality of death means that we must come to grips with the realities of life. Every moment is unique and passing. No person lives through his thirteenth year twice. No one has the opportunity to

HOW FREE ARE WE?

To use freedom well we have to do independent thinking. How free are we, really, to do what is best for ourselves? Free from the fads of the moment, the customs of the crowd?

94

see the same sunrise twice, or even the same cloud. Why waste your time on a television rerun, when reality only plays once?

Our environment faces us with realities, too, sometimes grim realities. Hurricanes and tornadoes, disease and starvation, earthquakes and floods—these are forms of brute force that operate against us. Only our own courageous action can overcome disaster.

As if that were not enough, human beings operate against one another. Violence strikes without reason; mobs overrun the innocent along with the guilty; dictators great and small, autocrats, and bullies destroy human dignity; and wars crush whole populations.

To the person who has religious awareness and has gathered up all the evidence, brute force is the greatest enemy—in whatever form it takes. Only the courage to act will help in the battle to overcome it.

Rabbi Akiba was nearly 80 years old when Simon bar Koziba [Bar Kochba] led a revolt against the Romans in Palestine. Akiba supported this cause of religious freedom, though he was too old to take up arms and fight. **A gentle defiance**

It would have been simple for Akiba to shrug his shoulders, to say that there was nothing that he could do about the Romans. After all, he was an old man. What could one old man do against the might of an empire?

But Akiba knew that it was not so! Only a slave would say such a thing—a man who had given up, who was no longer free to choose. The free person's responsibility was to stand and fight.

When the revolt was crushed, the Roman emperor made a new law forbidding the study of Torah and the practice of the Jewish religion. The emperor guessed that if the Jewish faith were destroyed, the people's desire for freedom would also be extinguished.

Akiba knew that the Roman was correct. Without Jewish learning, the people would be as helpless as a fish out of water.

He defied the law. Sitting in a public place, Akiba taught

the Torah to a group of students. For this, he was imprisoned. Three years later, the Romans ordered Akiba's execution. But during those three years, Akiba had continued to act courageously. From his prison cell he taught. He smuggled out answers to difficult questions of law to students who disguised themselves as peddlers walking beneath his jail window. And he taught Torah to all those who visited him in the prison.

The rest is not pleasant. One night, they came for Akiba and took him from the cell. All night they tortured him; but when the dawn came and with it the time to recite the Shema, Akiba did so.

The Roman officer in charge was astounded. "What are you?" he asked Akiba. "Are you a magician? Can you feel no pain?"

Akiba answered, "All my life I have waited to do this mitzvah properly. It is written, 'You shall love the Lord your God with all your heart, with all your soul, and with all your might.' I have always loved God with all my heart and all my might; and now I can love him with all my soul as well." And repeating the Shema, Rabbi Akiba died [Jerus. T., Ber. 14b].

(Although it is only a legend, one midrash tells us that

the Roman officer who tortured Akiba was so moved by Akiba's answer that he converted to Judaism.)

Akiba's expression of courage, the path that he explored through his religious awareness and his study, was that of teaching. His will was not to die, but to survive. As Sigmund Freud (1865–1939) put it, "It is the duty of every living creature to endure." **The triumph of freedom**

Akiba would not permit his own fear of death to keep him from doing the things that he felt would endure and last. He knew that justice would overcome injustice. And he was wise enough to see that he could not make peace with brute force, whether it was the force of nature of that of the Roman Empire.

Akiba also knew that a person does not become free by giving up freedom. As Rabbi Yohanan ben Zakkai said, "God can only be served by free moral agents; not by slaves" [Kid. 22b].

Our tradition does not ask of us to be more than human. The rabbis knew that humanity can be served only by leaders who are human. Even the Messiah would be a human being and not a God. **Reflection**

But our tradition does require of us that we overcome our tendencies to sidestep reality and to accept without question the values of the marketplace. These values are all around us, so much a part of us that we can almost forget them entirely. But occasions arise that cause us to face reality, and even the weakest among us must face death. The worth of our life is the sum total of our actions, our awareness, and our study.

As the clock strikes each hour, hope and faith are maintained not through waiting and delaying, but through action and courage. We each must bear the responsibility for what we do in the world, but our own worst enemies are always inside us finding excuses for not doing and for not acting. Ben Zoma said: "Who is mighty? He who rules over his Yetzer" [Avot 4:1].

10

The value of patience

You have probably heard people say that they are "frustrated." You may have even heard some speak of frustration as a kind of mental illness. Some psychologists believe that frustration is the most common form of mental illness in the United States today.

Being frustrated is something like being trapped. We become frustrated when the things we are doing or the things that we would like to do come to nothing; when they are thwarted, foiled, baffled, or defeated. Being frustrated means not being able to accomplish our goal.

Frustration can come about when we want to do something but don't do anything about it. But more often, it occurs even despite our best efforts. For example, you may do well in some or even most subjects, but constantly fail in one—biology, say. You try and try; you even memorize definitions and lists of life-support systems, but when the test grades are posted, you find that you have failed again. You become frustrated.

Frustration can be worse. You may even find yourself

frustrated by things totally beyond your control. For example, you may want very badly to be an airline stewardess or steward. But when you apply you find that you are not tall enough for the job. Or perhaps you want to become a commercial airline pilot, but your vision is not good enough. Letdowns and disappointments of these kinds can be frustrating.

There is a saying recorded in the Book of Ecclesiastes that the rabbis often quoted. It goes, "There is nothing new under the sun." This holds true of frustration, as it does of most things.

Frustration is not modern

The rabbis were aware of how people can become frustrated. Once Akiba was walking by the way and saw a corpse lying on the roadside far from any town. He dragged the corpse to the nearest cemetery and buried it there. But when he told this to the rabbis, they told him that what he had done was not according to the law. The law states that when a corpse is found in a strange place with no explanation, it is to be buried in that place. "I proceeded with all the best of intentions," Akiba said, "and I have sinned." From this we can see, the rabbis taught, how difficult it is to bring good intentions to fruition as noble achievements. Even the great Rabbi Akiba could be frustrated.

The rabbis did not consider frustration a disease. They thought of it rather as a mental attitude. If a person came to the study of Torah hoping to learn it all, for example, he could be greatly disappointed. For the study of Torah, even at the time of the rabbis, was known to be a lifelong task. Still, even a never-ending task has to be begun sometime. So the rabbis searched for a more positive attitude to help them in their task of long-term action.

They knew that the bringing about of the Days of the Messiah, the time to come in which peace and cooperation will join all humanity as one, was a long-term task. It meant that any person might not complete the work within his lifetime, that the work would have to be passed on from parent to children.

LOOKING FORWARD, ACTING NOW

Frustration is a part of human life. But striving and learning are still more important parts. The reward of today's effort is to be able to make a stronger effort tomorrow. The result of following the Law as far as we understand it is to learn still more of the Law.

The Jewish people relies not on one single individual or even on one single generation. Instead, we pass the task of upholding righteousness and peacemaking from generation to generation, hoping and trusting that some day the work will be completed, and the world will arrive at the End of Days, the Time of the Messiah.

Such work would all be very frustrating—especially in the face of such setbacks as war, poverty, and starvation—except that we have devised a special attitude that keeps our frustrations to a minimum. It is an attitude of faith and hope, an attitude of patience. Thus the rabbis taught that the time will come for each purpose and for every goal, if we work and if we trust.

A time for all things   The idea of a time for all things is not just that of the rabbis. It occurs even earlier. In the Book of Ecclesiastes, we can see it in its most poetic and specific form:

> There is a season for everything, a time for every occupation under heaven:
> A time for giving birth, a time for dying;
> A time for planting, a time for uprooting what has been planted.

A time for killing, a time for healing;
A time for knocking down, a time for building.
A time for tears, a time for laughter;
A time for mourning, a time for dancing.
A time for throwing stones away, a time for gathering them up;
A time for embracing, a time to refrain from embracing.
A time for searching, a time for losing;
A time for keeping, a time for throwing away.
A time for tearing, a time for sewing;
A time for keeping silent, a time for speaking.
A time for loving, a time for hating;
A time for war, a time for peace. [*Eccles. 3:1–8*]

This, then, is the attitude that we must hold with regard to all our actions: there is a time for all things, and each thing must come in its season. We have evidence already that this attitude can help us, for we have learned to be patient with nature.

We do not expect apples to grow in the summertime or peaches to ripen in the autumn. The farmer waits patiently for the time of sowing, the time of rain, the time of growing, and the time of harvest. We learn to expect snow in its season and heat in its time.

In the same way, the rabbis of Pirke Avot listed the seasons of our growing:

The seasons of man

At five years the age is reached for studying the Bible,
At ten for the study of Mishnah,
At thirteen for the doing of the commandments,
At eighteen for marriage,
At twenty for seeking a livelihood,
At thirty for entering into one's full strength,
At forty for understanding,
At fifty for wise advice,
At sixty to attain old age,
At seventy for the silver head,
At eighty the gift of special strength,
At ninety to bend beneath the weight of the years,
At a hundred to be as if already passed from the world.
[*Avot 5:24*]

Bar Mitzvah or Bat Mitzvah marks an important stage in life. You are now recognized—and recognize yourself—as mature enough to know and obey the Law. Awareness of Jewish values adds depth and beauty to any stage in life. And what is the most important time of life? The time you are living right now!

These are approximate times for each event and for each change in our life cycle. They are guideposts that give us an idea of what to expect as we grow and learn, as we build and change. The ages may not be the same in every time and place; still, they do not vary greatly.

But what can they teach us? Of what use are these "seasons of man" in helping us to avoid frustration and disappointment?

Taking your time Most of our frustrations fall into two categories: things that are frustrating because we cannot succeed at them, and things that are frustrating because we are not qualified for them. The first is like the knowledge of biology that seems constantly to escape us. The second is like the problem of the person who wishes to be a commercial airline pilot but has imperfect eyesight.

In both cases, the best attitude you can adopt is one of patience. Frustration is not always bad for us, nor is disappointment the end of the world. Often being frustrated or disappointed spurs us on to greater things. You may find, for example, that by redoubling your study efforts you become an excellent biology student and head on to a career as a doctor. Or you may find that piloting is not the only career in aviation that is interesting, challenging, and worthwhile.

This is true in terms of our Jewish way of life, too. It is difficult and frustrating to be a Jew. Acting out our Jewish beliefs and values very often brings us into conflict with the world around us. Being a Jew requires us to speak out when we see some wrong being committed, even when we know that our voice will make very little difference or even none at all. But we have faith that in time every good action will bear fruit.

We accept our disappointments and our frustrations, hoping that in the end what is good will survive and that the world will be a little better and a little brighter because we have lived in it. Even when we cannot see the fruit of our labors, we trust that what good we do will be established and useful.

From generation to generation

This is the moral of a story told in the Talmud regarding a certain saintly man by the name of Onias, also known as Honi:

One day, while walking along the road, Honi saw a man planting a carob tree and said to him, "Since a carob tree does not bear fruit for seventy years, are you certain of living so long as to eat the fruit of that tree you are planting?"

The man replied, "I found the world provided with carob trees because my forefathers planted them for me. I am planting them now for my sons." [Taanit 23a]

So, too, our actions must not only be judged in terms of the present, but we must also consider how they may affect the future. Today you may protest the building of a road across the Alaskan wilderness because of the effect that the road will certainly have upon Alaskan plant and wildlife in the future. Even if your protest is frustrated and the road built, you have not wasted your time. The roadbuilders may be just that much more careful because of what has been said, and perhaps future attempts to protect the wilderness will stand better chances for succeeding because people have already spoken out.

Rabbi Joshua and the Messiah

The rabbis knew that all real progress is made only one step at a time. In the Talmud they recorded a legend that illustrates the importance of this step-by-step approach to problem solving.

Students, weavers, farmers, orchard keepers—
mothers and teachers, too—all need to be patient
in their daily work. Who else would you say?
Fishermen? Scientists? Who does not need to be
patient through the years while working to help make
a better world?

Rabbi Joshua dreamed that he met Elijah the prophet. "When will the Messiah come?" he asked Elijah. "When will we be relieved of the burden of Rome?"

Elijah replied, "Go and ask the Messiah himself."

Surprised, Joshua said, "Where may I find the Messiah?"

"At the main gate of Rome," said Elijah.

"And how will I know him?"

"The Messiah sits among the beggars of the city as they nurse their wounds and sores. Each morning the beggars come and unwrap the bandages exposing their wounds to the healing rays of the sun. The Messiah comes there too and sits among the beggars. But the Messiah loosens only one bandage at a time. For he thinks: 'If I am called, I must waste no time.' And so, the Messiah unties first one bandage exposing one sore to healing, then ties it up again and uncovers another sore."

Without warning Joshua found himself at the gate to the city of Rome. It did not take him long to recognize the Messiah for only one beggar did not moan and bewail his lot, and only one beggar loosened the bandages one at a time.

"Greetings to thee, my Master and Teacher," Joshua said to the beggar.

"Greetings to thee, Joshua ben Levi," the Messiah replied.

"When will you see fit to come?" Joshua asked.

"Why, today," the Messiah answered. And, as the beggar answered, Rabbi Joshua was transported to his home, as if by magic.

All day Joshua waited to rejoice at the news of the coming of the Messiah, but as night fell his disappointment grew until it knew no bounds.

The next morning, Joshua was awakened by the prophet Elijah.

"The Messiah has spoken untruthfully," Joshua said bitterly. "He said that he would come 'today' but 'today' has come and gone and the Messiah has not come."

Elijah smiled. "The Messiah meant to say: 'Today, if today you would hear my voice." [Sanh. 98a]

It is a strange legend indeed—a Messiah who speaks in riddles, a rabbi who travels magically from Palestine to Rome and back, conversations with Elijah long dead. In a way, it is more than a legend, it is almost a puzzle of events.

About the Messiah

The simplest lesson to be learned is the lesson that Elijah teaches at the end: the Messiah is always ready to come, it is we who must prepare ourselves and play our parts in bringing him here.

Of course, the rabbis understood the Messiah to be a figure of legend. They even held that the Messiah will come only when we no longer need him. That is, the Messiah will come when we have brought the world to near-perfection on our own, through our own work. Then, whoever rules over that time of peace would indeed be the Messiah!

Studying the puzzle

Why should the Messiah be a beggar? Why should he be found at the gate of the city? Why should the city be Rome? Why should the Messiah's body be covered with sores and wounds? Why have the rabbis kept this story in the Talmud?

Let us begin with why the Messiah is a beggar, why he is in Rome, and why at the gate of the city. In ancient days, the gate of the city was where its marketplace was located. Here the farmers came and opened their stalls and the merchants their outdoor shops. The marketplace is the perfect place to find the Messiah waiting—for here is everything that the Messiah is not, and yet everything in the marketplace could become transformed if only we would work to change it. We spoke in the preceding chapter of the "values of the marketplace." Now you can see that the figure of the beggar-Messiah represents the Jewish people among the other nations of the world.

And Rome stands for those nations. What Rome cherished is not what the Jews cherished. For example, we respect learning and wisdom above all things—therefore our greatest heroes are not generals or emperors, but teachers and sages. The values of Rome are the "values of the marketplace."

The deeper meaning Why is the Messiah covered with sores and wounds? And what is behind his mysterious action of loosening one bandage at a time? We have already learned that he wished to be ready to go at once when he was called. But there is also another meaning.

One of the great strengths of the Jewish people has been our attention to the details of living together. The Talmud and most of the codes that have been built upon it pay the closest attention to every small problem of daily life. Each of these problems is like a small sore infecting the body of the Jewish people, and our attitude is to deal with them step by step, loosening the bandages one at a time, studying each sore and trying to heal it before going on to the next. We do not always answer every problem, but we try.

Here again the Messiah may be seen as a symbol for the Jewish people, as he prepares himself for his coming by healing each small sore one at a time. But, you may ask, isn't it better to think of the large things and forget about the details?

Actually, it works the other way around. A good example is chapter 19 in the Book of Leviticus. We call this chapter "The Holiness Code," because in it we are commanded, "Be holy, for I, the Lord your God, am Holy" [Lev. 19:2]. Of all the commandments in this chapter of Leviticus, the commandment to be holy is far and away the

greatest and the most important. But in order to understand it and follow it, we need details: what exactly does it
mean to "be holy"?

It means, "You must not hold back a laborer's wage,
even until the next morning." It means, "You must not
curse the dumb, nor put a stumbling block in the blind
man's way." It means, "You must not practice fortune-
telling or magic." It means, "You are not to tattoo yourselves." It means, "You are to rise up before the grey-
haired; you are to honor old age and fear your God" [Lev.
19:32]. This is what is meant by the command to be holy.
The concerns of Judaism reach into every action, every
dealing that one person has with another.

The key to the story lies in the way the Messiah is waiting:
he does not waste his time, but uses it to heal his sores and
wounds—to improve himself through action. He knows
that he must wait until all people are prepared to listen to
the voice of the Messiah, but in the meantime he acts in a
positive way, a way that saves him from frustration. As
Rabbi Tarphon said:

**The Messiah
and waiting**

הַיּוֹם קָצֵר. וְהַמְּלָאכָה מְרֻבָּה. וְהַפּוֹעֲלִים עֲצֵלִים. וְהַשָּׂכָר
הַרְבֵּה. וּבַעַל הַבַּיִת דּוֹחֵק:

*The day is short, and the work is great, the laborers are slow, but
the reward is much and the Master is urgent. [Avot 2:20]*

That is, we have limited time to do what is good and right
in this world, and the work is so great that time is very
precious. We are slow and lazy and we have to learn to
overcome our natural tendency to waste time. But when we
work with all our hearts, there is blessing in our work—we
are often rewarded by seeing what we have done even if
we may not experience its full fruition. But why is God, the
Master, urgent? Because "now" is really the only time we
ever have. As Hillel said, "If not now, when?"

It is important to understand this concept of the rabbis'
teaching. Being patient and being active can be two sides

WHO IS WAITING?
WHO IS READY?

We Jews believe in working while waiting for the Messiah. But according to this legend, who is really waiting all the while?

of the same coin. While we wait, we do not have to stand still. If we do, we are sure to be frustrated as a result of our inactivity just as we will be frustrated if we merely keep on doing and doing without thoughtful waiting.

You might compare the person who just keeps acting without stopping with the rear wheel of a car stuck in the mud. The engine of the car roars and roars, the driver keeps pressing down on the gas pedal, but all the wheel can do is keep spinning without taking hold: it really is going nowhere.

With patience, the active kind of Jewish waiting, a person learns to make adjustments one at a time, step by step.

In the situation described above, consider the driver who gets out, studies the problem, finds a board to place beneath the rear wheel, and slowly moves the car forward and the wheel out of the ditch.

Instant results?

Still, you cannot always expect instant results. You may patiently study the problem, decide that a board under the wheel will solve it, and then find that the mud is too watery—that the board is too small and merely sinks into the mire. Then you might feel disappointed or frustrated. You may feel like kicking the tire. (You have to watch out for that Yetzer HaRa—it's always trying to sneak up on you!) But the best attitude is to persevere, to go on trying, patiently.

The same Rabbi Tarphon whom we quoted above also said:

לֹא עָלֶיךָ הַמְּלָאכָה לִגְמֹר. וְלֹא אַתָּה בֶן־חוֹרִין לְהִבָּטֵל מִמֶּנָּה.

It is not your duty to complete the work, but neither are you free to desist from it. [Avot 2:21]

We do not always get to see the results of all our actions. That is no reason for not beginning. Just because we may not live to eat the fruit of the tree we plant today is not a reason not to plant.

Reflection   We learn to overcome frustration when we learn to expect each thing in its proper season. In overcoming frustration and disappointment, we make our world seem brighter, for we begin concentrating on what is good, even when it is something small, and we begin appreciating what is important, even when it is merely a detail in a much larger picture.

The importance of the work we do lies in *what* we do, not in how much we do. It is not our duty to finish every task that we begin, but we must begin if the task is ever to be completed. When we choose, along with the Jewish people, to bring closer the time of the Messiah—to show through our actions that we are ready for a time of peace, a time when everyone will love others as himself—we choose to undertake a task that we may not ever see completed. That does not make the task less worthy.

Every day is a good day to begin the task of bringing the Messiah. Every day is a good day to look carefully at the things we do and to try to do things that will help. Every day is a good day to loosen one bandage, look at one imperfection, and see just how much we can do to make it better.

11

The value of love

Pirke Avot contains the record of an unusual homework assignment given by Rabbi Yohanan ben Zakkai to his five students, all rabbis themselves. It consisted of two questions:

> Go forth and see which is the good way to which a person should hold [and] . . . which is the evil way which a person should avoid. [Avot 2:13–14]

In saying "Go forth," Yohanan was telling the students to seek their answers outside the classroom, in the world of everyday action.

Before you go on to read the answers that the five student rabbis gave to Yohanan's assignment, perhaps you should take out a pen and paper and write down in a few words your own answers. What do you think is the key to doing justice and righteousness? What thing do you think must be avoided if we are to avoid evil?

The answers The answers of the five student rabbis form a kind of summary of the first half of our study in this book. Many of the ideas that we have placed together in this unit on how to prepare ourselves for Jewish action are contained in the short answers the rabbis gave. Some of these ideas are probably contained in the short answers that you wrote down, too. See how close you came to the ways that we have studied. How would you answer these questions?

The answers of Rabbi Eliezer Eliezer was a student with a spongelike memory. His teacher had called him "a cemented cistern" because like a cistern that holds every drop of water poured into it, Eliezer remembered every teaching of Torah he had ever heard. How would such a person answer the two questions?

Rabbi Eliezer said that the good way to hold to is "a good eye," and that the evil way to avoid is "an evil eye."

We can easily understand what is meant by "an evil eye." It is a way of looking at the world and seeing an ugly, unhappy, miserable place to live. The evil eye stands for envy, jealousy, constant complaining, and unhappiness.

A man once appeared before his rabbi and said, "I am finished with this business of being good. All my life people have said that if I was good I would succeed. But look, here I have a list of twenty names of people who were evil and successful. Now I am going to cheat my customers and I will be rich, too."

The rabbi smiled. "I see your list of those who were evil and succeeded," he said. "But where is your list of those who were good and succeeded?"

When a person looks at the world through an evil eye, he naturally sees only that which is evil and he is disturbed by everything.

It is just the opposite for a person with "a good eye." The world seen through a good eye is a place of joy and cheer, of satisfaction and contentment. The good eye is our religious awareness, our ability to see what good can be brought into the world through us.

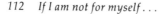

SEEKING RIGHTLY, CHOOSING WELL

What was the man with the "evil eye" looking for when he brought that list to "his rabbi?" What should he have been looking for? Still, do we want to see only good where evil actually appears? If so, how could we be wise and avoid the evil friend, as Rabbi Joshua advises?

Eliezer's answer, then, tells us that much of what we see really depends on the way we look at things.

The Proverbs say, "He who has a good eye will be blessed, for he gives of his bread to the poor" [Prov. 22:9]. In other words, even if a person with "a good eye" is himself poor, he will find someone poorer to give charity to, because his good eye allows him to see himself as rich.

The good way to follow, according to Rabbi Joshua, is "a good friend," and the evil way to shun is "an evil friend."

Rabbi Joshua's answers

Rabbi Joshua's answer may remind you of the adage "One rotten apple will spoil the bunch." His idea, however, was not too far from others expressed elsewhere in Avot—for example:

נִתַּי הָאַרְבֵּלִי אוֹמֵר. הַרְחֵק מִשָּׁכֵן רָע. וְאַל תִּתְחַבֵּר לְרָשָׁע.

Nittai the Arbelite, said, Keep yourself far from an evil neighbor, do not associate with the wicked. [Avot 1:7]

Zadok and Hillel agreed that a person should not separate himself from the community; and it was also taught that we should separate ourselves from those who do evil.

You probably know the "rotten apple" type. He is the one who says, "Let's steal this magazine, the storekeeper will never miss it." The rotten apple says, "Let's skip school just one day. What a time we can have!" The rotten apple is the one who sets you thinking that maybe these things are not so bad after all. Other people do them and get away with them—why not you? The rotten apple is the one who speaks directly to your Yetzer HaRa.

To Joshua the worst path to follow is the path this evil companion leads you on. The best path is the path of good friendship and community. When the friends we choose are those who are good in their ways, we become more like them. We also become ourselves good friends to others and lead them down the right path. Joshua was like this himself. He was a blessing to all who knew him.

He who leads many people to righteousness, through him no sin shall occur; but he who leads many people to sin, shall not be given the means to repent. [Avot 5:21]

Rabbi Yose's answers

Rabbi Yose's answers are very similar to those of Rabbi Joshua. Yose answered that the good path to follow is "a good neighbor," the evil path "an evil neighbor." There would be no difference really between a good friend and a good neighbor except if we think in terms of the community. And that is the distinction Rabbi Yose is making.

A good neighbor is concerned with what can be done by the group working together. A good neighbor is careful of the way his lawn is kept and of how he disposes of his garbage—in general, he is considerate of the feelings of the people who live around him. Being a good neighbor means developing a kind of attitude toward others that stresses concern: concern for the welfare of all the people in the neighborhood, concern for the future of the community, concern for the way of life that the community chooses. Such concerns are the signs of a good neighbor.

What marks the evil neighbor is selfishness. One of the greatest harms that the Yetzer HaRa can accomplish is to turn a person into an evil neighbor. While others take pride in their community, the evil neighbor looks out only for himself. When the community is in danger or falls on bad times the evil neighbor simply moves on, seeking for his comfort in another community. We occasionally hear of a neighborhood "going bad" or becoming a difficult place to live in. Usually this occurs because the people in the neighborhood have stopped being good neighbors to one another, have begun to act in the manner of the evil neighbor, caring only for themselves.

Rabbi Simeon's answers to Yoḥanan's questions were different entirely. Simeon said that the good way is followed by "the one who considers the results" of his actions.

Rabbi Simeon's answers

הרואה את
הנולד

A person who uses his religious awareness to help him see what might result if he behaves in a certain way will be less likely to make mistakes that will harm others. People do not usually intend to act cruelly, but they often act without thinking. For example, we often allow our anger to get the better of us and insult others whom we really care for. Considering in advance the pain that such behavior can cause others will normally keep us from expressing our anger in this way.

Then, too, in order to "consider the results" of our actions, we usually have to gather evidence before acting. For us this means studying the outcome or the possible outcomes. When we study the possible outcomes of our actions in advance, we are more likely to act kindly, because we see how our actions may harm others—and even, in the long run, ourselves.

The story is told of an old man who in his last years came to live with his son's family. Now, his son was afraid that his old father would break the good china if he were allowed to eat from it. So the son prepared for the older man a wooden bowl and wooden spoon with which to eat.

Now, one day the son came home and saw his own child carving up a piece of wood with a knife.

"What are you doing?" he asked the child.

"I am making a wooden bowl for you to eat from when you are as old as grandfather," the child said.

Simeon's answer to the second question was that a person should avoid being "one who borrows but does not repay." At first, this does not seem to be the opposite of "considering the results" of one's actions, yet in a very real sense it is. For a person who borrows without thinking of

BEING RESPONSIBLE

Rabbi Yose said that the good way was that of the good neighbor; the evil way that of the evil neighbor. Rabbi Simeon said that the good way was to consider the results of one's actions, and that one should not be a person who borrows but does not repay. What do these two sets of answers mean in terms of being responsible?

repayment is certainly not considering the results of his action.

The rabbis taught that we should respect the property of others as if it were our own. When we borrow something, then, we should treat it as carefully as we do our own belongings.

Rabbi Simeon went on to explain that when we borrow from another person, we are like one "who borrows from God." In the final analysis, all things which we own are "borrowed from God." Giving charity, then, is a kind of repayment for what we have borrowed. As it is written in the Psalms, "The wicked borrows and pays not again, but the righteous deals graciously and gives" [Psalms 37:21].

The last answers were those given by Rabbi Eleazar ben Arach. Eleazar said that the way to follow is the way of "a good heart," and that the evil way to shun is the way of "an evil heart."

The answers of Rabbi Eleazar

After he had listened to his students' answers, Rabbi Yoḥanan said to them: I approve most of the [answers] of Eleazar ben Arach, . . . for in his words, yours are included [Avot 2:13, 14].

The idea of a good heart is perhaps the best way to sum up the unit of study we are now completing. All things enter into the idea of having a good heart—all the qualities of the kind of person it is possible for each of us to be. The person with a good heart sees the good that is all around him and adds to it through his own actions. The person with the good heart tries to live in the image of God and to do honor to others.

A good example is one of the favorite sayings of the rabbis:

I am a creature [of God] and my neighbor is also His creature. My work is in the city and his is in the field. I rise early to my work, and he rises early to his. As he cannot excel in my work, so I cannot excel in his work. But perhaps you say, I do great things and he does small things. We have learnt that it matters not whether a man does much or little, if only he directs his heart to heaven. [Ber. 17a]

Rabbi Eleazar said the way to follow is the way of
"a good heart," the way to shun the way of "an evil
heart." How does having a good heart include
(1) having a good eye? (2) being a good friend?
(3) being a good neighbor? (4) considering the results
of one's actions?

**The path of
the good heart** We might call this teaching "the path of the good heart." It
is as true today as it was when the rabbis taught it in the
academy at Yavneh. It matters not whether you become a
physician or a laborer, a chef or a clerk, a policeman or a
storekeeper; what makes a person great is following the
path of the good heart.

*A person may say, I have not learned to be wise, I have not studied
the Law, what am I to do?*

But God said to the Israelites, All wisdom and all the Law is a single easy thing: the one who fears Me, and does the Law has all the wisdom and all the Law in his heart. [Deut. R. 11:6]

And to show that all the Law is found in *doing*, the rabbis taught that the last letter of the Torah is a *lamed*, and the first letter is a *bet*. Set side by side these spell the word לֵב, which means "heart." This is to show that all that is contained in the Torah, the Law of Israel, is contained in the heart of each Jew.

Reflection

We must each find an answer to the question posed by Hillel: "If I am not for myself, who will be for me?"

Our tradition alone cannot teach us the answer to this question, for the answer is closer—it is in each of our hearts. What our tradition can teach us is what it means to be *for* yourself, and who will be *for* you when you act for yourself.

Hillel's question is a hundred questions in one: If I am not myself, who will be me? If I do not take part in my community, who in the community will take my part for me? If I do not take a stand in my own name, who will fight for what I believe? If I do not work to make myself better, who will do that work for me? If I do not direct my actions, who will direct them for me? And more.

What our tradition does teach us is that we can become good through our actions, that becoming good is not so difficult to achieve, and that the reward for being good is the good that results. So the person who wants to act *for* himself will act *for* others, too. The commandment of the Torah "Love your neighbor as yourself" means that you must first love yourself in order to love others.

A rabbi was once teaching what was meant when the Torah said, Love your neighbor as yourself. He turned to one student and asked, "Do you love me?"

The student thought for a minute and then replied honestly, "I think I do."

"Then tell me what causes me pain," the rabbi said.

"I do not know what causes you pain," the student replied.

"Then you do not love me," the rabbi said. "To love someone means to know what causes him pain."

Each of us knows what hurts us and when we hurt. When we love ourselves, we try to keep ourselves from being hurt so that we will not cause ourselves pain. Only when we understand the meaning of pain do we begin to understand how others feel. That is why Hillel's questioning does not end with "If I am not for myself, who will be for me?" Hillel goes on to say, "And if I am only for myself, what am I? And if not now, when?" If a person is only for himself, if he is so selfish as to think that he is the only one who matters, he loses all meaning. It is a way of sidestepping reality, the coward's way out of true loving. Cowards do not love themselves.

Hillel's question "If I am not for myself, who will be for me?" means that we must value ourselves and our possibilities, that we must train ourselves to act with self-respect. If we do, we will have a basis for acting properly

toward others, for respecting them as we respect ourselves. Just as we strive to create an inner balance between what is good and generous and what is bad or selfish, so too we must try to create an inner balance between consideration of ourselves and of our neighbors. We must love one another.

And just as the Jewish tradition helps us to train ourselves to be better and to find reasons to love ourselves in the kinds of actions that we take, so it helps us to train ourselves to live with other people. Each of us trying to follow the path of the good heart must together build a society in which we all try to avoid causing pain to one another. We must build a society in which the community follows the path of the good heart because all the members of the community are good as individuals.

This is the essence of what we will study in the next unit, as we try to answer Hillel's second question: "If I am only for myself, what am I?"

Among the Jews of the city of Nikolsburg in Moravia a strange custom prevailed. Each new rabbi was asked to write down a regulation in the chronicles of the congregation, and the Jews would follow it in honor of their rabbi from that time on.

Rabbi Shmelke was asked to take the position of rabbi and told of the custom. Day after day the curious folk would look into the chronicle, but the new rabbi had not written in his regulation. Instead, Rabbi Shmelke spent his time looking at each and every member of the congregation and waiting.

Time and again the members looked to the open book, waiting. And time and again Rabbi Shmelke would study the people, waiting.

Finally, as the High Holy Days approached, the folk came to speak to their new rabbi and told him that there was no time for further delay. "We are anxious to follow our custom," they explained to him.

Then Rabbi Shmelke went to the back of the synagogue where the chronicle was kept and wrote in it the Ten Commandments.

12

The value of community

הִלֵּל אוֹמֵר. אַל תִּפְרוֹשׁ מִן הַצִּבּוּר.

Hillel said, Separate not yourself from the community. [Avot 2:5]

To live alone

Our community is like a living organism. It is difficult to imagine our tradition treating each person separately from the community as a whole. Just as with a single body, when the foot is amputated, the body misses it, but the body continues to live; whereas the foot withers and dies.

As babies, we need parents to care for us. As young children, we must be taught by others to walk and to talk. As we grow further, we rely upon one another for advice and counsel. In sickness, we need others to help us recover and to care for us. And in old age, we look to others for aid. It is clear that we are not meant to live without our community.

Once in a northern country, a gloriously colored bird alighted atop the tallest tree and nested in its leaves. The king of the country was told of the unusual bird and asked that feathers be brought to him so that he might see them. The people decided to make a living ladder to reach the bird. One stood upon the shoulders of another until they had almost succeeded.

But it took a long time to build the human ladder and those who stood nearest the ground lost patience, shook themselves free, and everything collapsed. [Baal Shem Tov]

Jewish society is like the living ladder in this story. Our goals are difficult to reach—goals of peace, justice, mercy, and righteousness. Still, we know that they are worth trying to reach, and being part of the community helps us to reach them.

We need one another Our lives are so complex that each of us are in need of many other people of differing skills to help us.

Ben Zoma once saw a gathering of people on the Temple Mount. He said, "Blessed is He . . . who has created all these people to serve me."

He explained: What labor Adam had to carry out before he had bread to eat! He ploughed, he sowed, he reaped, he bound the sheaves, he threshed and winnowed, he selected the ears, he ground them, he sifted the flour, he kneaded and baked, and then at last he ate; whereas I get up, and find all these things done for me.

And how many labors Adam had to carry out before he obtained a garment to wear! He had to shear, wash the wool, comb it, spin it, weave it, and then at last he obtained a garment; whereas I get up and find all these things done for me. [Ber. 58a]

This joining of talents—tanner, doctor, lawyer, sailor, soldier, merchant, gardener, and poet—is one of the great accomplishments of human beings. How many things are done for us—and how many things we do for others! No matter what your chosen profession, you will contribute to a kind of living ladder reaching upward toward a better society.

All are important Every occupation is important to the community. A well-digger once saw Rabbi Yohanan ben Zakkai walking by and called out, "Ho there, Rabbi. Did you know that I am as important as you?"

"Why is that?" Yohanan asked.

"Well," the well digger said, mopping his brow with a cloth, "it is because my work is as important to our community as yours. You see, when you tell a man or a woman to go to the ritual baths and cleanse themselves, it is I who provide the water for them." [Eccles. R. 4:17]

No profession is so lowly that the person who follows it cannot make a contribution to the common good. In ancient times, shepherding was considered to be among the lowliest professions. Tending his flock all day and all night, without care or ambition, the shepherd was little respected by the community.

Yet Moses was a shepherd. And the Midrash tells us that it was Moses' concern for the stray sheep that made him fit to lead the Jewish people out of Egypt.

The rabbis had various occupations, too: Hillel was a woodcutter and Shammai was a mason, Abba Hoshaya was a laundryman, Rabbi Joshua and Rabbi Isaac Napaha were both blacksmiths, and rabbis Ḥisda and Pappa were brewers. Other rabbis were farmers, tradesmen, and craftsmen. They were members of all social classes. And all this was in addition to their studies and teaching!

TO EACH HIS OWN

The skills and labor of many different kinds of workers make the community possible. Judaism teaches the dignity of all labor and enjoins respect for the laborer.

A ladder in time The community is greater than any single individual because the community supports all. Einstein relied for his bread upon the same farmer as those who lived in Einstein's community and were not so famous.

This is especially true of the Jewish community because its members think of it in a special way. We are not just a group of people who are members of a particular synagogue, or the Jews who live in this city or that town. We are not just the Jews who live in this country, or even the Jews who live in different countries all around the world. We are a community in time. And the ladder we are building is a ladder in time. The base of the ladder is Abraham, and the rungs just above are Sarah, Isaac, Rebecca, Jacob, Leah, and Rachel; then, in time, our teacher Moses. The ladder itself is traced in the first verse of the first chapter of Avot:

מֹשֶׁה קִבֵּל תּוֹרָה מִסִּינַי. וּמְסָרָהּ לִיהוֹשֻׁעַ. וִיהוֹשֻׁעַ לִזְקֵנִים. וּזְקֵנִים לִנְבִיאִים. וּנְבִיאִים מְסָרוּהָ לְאַנְשֵׁי כְנֶסֶת הַגְּדוֹלָה:

Moses received the Torah on Sinai, and handed it down to Joshua; Joshua to the elders; the elders to the prophets; the prophets to the Men of the Great Assembly. [Avot 1:1]

Whether the ladder will reach the End of Days depends on our patience and our diligence. We are not born atop the ladder. We must climb it rung by rung, learning and studying, working and striving, until we reach our place in time—and then holding on and passing the heritage on to our children.

For the sake of heaven All this striving would hardly be necessary if there were no goal, no end in sight. And there is a goal. It is making a reality of the dreams of the Prophets, a world that is based on the law of the Torah, the law of the mitzvot, a world in which each person is kind and just, treating others fairly and creating peace.

וְכָל הָעוֹסְקִים עִם הַצִּבּוּר יִהְיוּ עוֹסְקִים עִמָּהֶם לְשֵׁם שָׁמַיִם. שֶׁזְּכוּת אֲבוֹתָם מְסַיַּעְתָּם. וְצִדְקָתָם עוֹמֶדֶת לָעַד.

Let all who work for the community, the people, work with them
for the sake of Heaven, for the merit of their fathers sustains them,
and their righteousness endures forever. [Avot 2:2]

In the entire book of Pirke Avot, the only thing we are
asked to do "for the sake of Heaven" is to work on behalf of
our community.

But what kind of work is intended? What kinds of action
must we take?

Just as we earlier emphasized that a person must love
himself *before* he can love others ("Love your neighbor *as*
yourself"), so we now turn our attention to the fact that a
person must *also* love others.

Loving your
neighbor

It is told that Abraham would greet all travelers, whether friends or
strangers, with open arms, welcoming them into his tent. We are even
told that Abraham built his tent in the center of a crossroads with
doors on every side, so that a passerby coming from any direction
would come directly into Abraham's tent.

It was Abraham's custom to wash the feet of the traveler (a gesture
of friendship among desert peoples), and to feed the traveler. Then,
when the traveler would thank Abraham for his hospitality and his
meal, Abraham would say, "Nay, do not thank me, but thank the
Lord." The traveler would ask, "Who is this Lord?" And so Abraham
would tell each traveler of the one God who created Heaven and earth
and all that is therein.

Once an old man came to the door of Abraham's tent and Abraham
welcomed him as always, washing his feet and preparing for the old
man a meal. But after the meal, when Abraham asked the old man to
thank the Lord for the blessing of food, the old man replied that he
worshipped only fire, and would thank no other god but the god of
flame and ash.

Then Abraham was angered and drove the old man out of his tent
and into the cold desert night. At once a voice came to Abraham
saying, "Wherefore have you done this thing? For seventy years I
have suffered this old man, and you cannot suffer him even for one
night!"

So Abraham chased after the old man and brought him back to the
tent and kept him there for the night. [Benjamin Franklin, based on
Gen. R. 43:8]

It is a Jewish value that all people are loved by God and are holy, whether sinner or saint.

Ransoming the captive One of the most sacred duties of a Jewish community is helping those who are kidnapped and held for ransom. In Jewish law, paying a ransom to captors is placed above even the duties of clothing and feeding the poor.

At the time the Mishnah was compiled, kidnapping was used as a means of raising money, and Jews were kidnapped frequently to be held for ransom. Finally, in order to discourage kidnappers from making great profits from their evil, the rabbis limited the amount that could be paid a kidnapper.

Captives should not be ransomed for more than their value, as a precaution for the general good. [Mishnah, Git. 4:6]

Still, debate always arose over the "value" of a specific captive.

Kidnapping has not disappeared from the world scene. If anything, we have seen more of it in recent years. Today, whole communities of Jews can be held captive for ransom, while other Jewish communities work and pray for their rescue, raising ransom money through donations and gifts.

The ransoming of the land of Israel has prepared the way for all of the great ransoms and rescues of modern times. Countless millions of dollars have been spent in the effort to redeem the remnants of European Jewry after the Holocaust.

Gemilut Ḥasadim The ransoming of captives is an act of *Gemilut Ḥasadim.* There is no real way of translating this Hebrew phrase, yet within its two words are the key to the Jewish conception of community. Gemilut Ḥasadim is lovingkindness. Gemilut Ḥasadim is benevolence. Gemilut Ḥasadim is an act of kindness done without thought or hope of reward. Gemilut Ḥasadim is a kind of charity, though not in the usual sense.

WORK FOR THE COMMUNITY

We may work for our community by being diligent in our occupations, by laboring in the Torah, by being hospitable to wayfarers (as Abraham was), and by many acts of concern and lovingkindness.

Greater is Gemilut Ḥasadim than the giving of charity in three respects—the giving of charity is performed with money and Gemilut Ḥasadim with personal service or money; the giving of charity is restricted to the poor and Gemilut Ḥasadim can be displayed to poor and rich; the giving of charity is restricted to the living, and Gemilut Ḥasadim can be given to both living and dead. [Suk. 49b]

Gemilut Ḥasadim is made up of all the kindly acts that we do for one another in order to sweeten our human relationships and to make our community a more pleasant one for all who live in it.

Almost everything that we have spoken about in the preceding unit was just to prepare us for this Jewish concept of Gemilut Ḥasadim. For once we realize the value of life and the nature of our own free choice, our religious awareness urges us to do what is right—just for the sake of doing good. That is the essence of Gemilut Ḥasadim.

In preparation

In Avot we are taught—

Gemilut Ḥasadim and attitude

יְהִי בֵיתְךָ פָּתוּחַ לָרְוָחָה. וְיִהְיוּ עֲנִיִּים בְּנֵי בֵיתֶךָ.

Let your house be open wide and let the poor be members of your household. [Avot 1:5]

Still, Gemilut Ḥasadim has less to do with the act than with the attitude behind the act.

It happened once that Solomon found himself carried far from home by one of the four winds of evil and deposited in a strange land. The dust and dirt caked his robes and made them seem more the rags of a beggar than the clothing of a king. And as dusk fell and he went from house to house searching for a meal and a place to stay the night, he found that the people ignored him and thought him nothing more than a common beggar. When he argued, "I am Solomon, King of Israel," they laughed at him and replied mockingly, "If so, we are all Queens of Sheba!"

At last, weary and starving, Solomon came to the house of a merchant who had traveled far and wide. "You are the King of Israel," the merchant said. "I have often seen your face as you marched in a parade." Then the merchant invited Solomon to come in and dine with him.

"My, my, but it is a terrible shame," the merchant began as the appetizer was being served. "Look how you have become nothing more than a commoner. What has become of your riches and your gold? Where is your palace and all your slaves?" So it was with the soup. "My, my." And with the salad, "It's a terrible shame." With the main course, it was "What a pity. My, my, what a pity." And Solomon found that he could not eat for the tears that rolled down his cheeks and dropped onto his plate.

The next night Solomon was offered a meal by a poor woodcutter. "I have not much to offer," the woodcutter said, "but here is bread enough for us to share and a pot of meal freshly cooked." Slowly, as they ate, Solomon told his story, and the woodcutter would respond, "I am sure that all will be for the best." Or, "Tomorrow is yet another day, things may seem brighter then." And slowly Solomon's mood changed, too. He grew more and more like himself and felt again that he was indeed Solomon, the King of Israel.

When the evil wind saw that Solomon could not be defeated, he [that is, the wind] was forced to take Solomon back to Israel, where all—the merchant who was kind in a cruel way, and the woodcutter who was kind in a pleasant way—seemed as if in a dream. [Sefer HaAggadah]

Another example of how Gemilut Hasadim can be displayed equally by rich or by poor, to the rich or to the poor, is found in the commandment to visit the sick. Once Rabbi Akiba heard that one of his students had fallen ill and that no one had gone to visit him. Immediately, Akiba went to the home of the sick student and cleaned the room and cheered up the invalid. Then the student said to him, "You have restored me to life" [Ned. 40a].

Rich or poor

What Rabbi Akiba had really done was to bring the student back into the group, to assure the ailing fellow that he was not forgotten when he was not around. Helping others to feel wanted by visiting them when they are sick is a mitzvah—and an act of Gemilut Hasadim.

Visiting the sick is also an act of personal service and is a good example of how Gemilut Hasadim is not dependent on money alone. Of course, we can use money for Gemilut Hasadim, but it is not always necessary, or even best. Working in behalf of the community, either through some private organization or through the government itself, is considered to be an act of Gemilut Hasadim. If a person does it with the proper spirit, his true reward will be found not among the community, but in his partnership with God, who rules the earth with His heavenly government.

Personal service

> Let all who work for the community, the people, work with them for the sake of heaven, for then the merit of their fathers sustains them, and their righteousness endures forever. [Avot 2:2]

What does this passage mean by "the merit of their fathers?" This refers again to the ladder in time that we are building, for the "fathers" here are Abraham, Isaac, and Jacob. It is said that no matter how low a Jew is bent, he or she can always call to God in the name of our fathers, Abraham, Isaac, and Jacob.

When we give our personal service to community, we are climbing the ladder in time and helping others—not for any reward, but "for the sake of Heaven."

The living and the dead   Finally, Gemilut Ḥasadim is greater than charity because it can be extended to the dead as well as to the living, while charity affects only the living. This is another way of saying that we are serving for no reward when we help to prepare a body for the grave, or prepare a grave to receive a corpse, or when we treat a dead body with the proper amount of respect.

The Jewish community has always been very conscious of this particular duty and has everywhere established Jewish graveyards and societies for burial. Even today, in every synagogue there is a committee that stands ready to help when someone dies.

Acts of lovingkindness   What sets the Jewish community apart is our constant concern with Gemilut Ḥasadim—acts of lovingkindness. The ways in which we treat one another with respect and kindness reflect the ways in which we think about ourselves.

ATTITUDES

Our attitudes matter, too. How is the strength of our community extended to captives? To the sick, absent from their daily activities? On what basis was the poor merchant able to cheer up King Solomon?

Once as Rabban Yoḥanan ben Zakkai was coming out of Jerusalem, Rabbi Joshua followed after him and saw the temple in ruins.

"Woe unto us," Rabbi Joshua cried, "that this place where we atoned for our sins through sacrifices is now laid waste!"

"My son," Rabban Yoḥanan said to him, "be not grieved; we have another atonement as effective as this. And what is it? It is Gemilut Ḥasadim, as it is said, 'For I desire mercy and not sacrifice' (Hos. 6:6)." [ARN 4]

Separating yourself from the community robs you of your heritage. It weakens you as an individual and forces you to selfish thoughts and actions. Living together in the community forces us to think about the wants and needs of others and helps us to keep our Yetzer HaRa under control.

You can rob yourself of your heritage in yet another way when you separate yourself from the community, for you weaken the ladder in time that our community has been building. We all then lose the chance to reach out and touch the beautiful bird in the nest just beyond reach, the brightly plumed Bird of Paradise that is within our grasp if only we dream and act in unison.

You can see from as simple an example as the ransoming of captives the great work that may be done by the Jewish community with concerted effort. And you should come to think of the community as a kind of tool that helps you build what you could not build otherwise: a world filled with righteousness and acts of lovingkindness.

No wonder Hillel said, "Separate not yourself from the community."

13

The value of possessions

אַרְבַּע מִדּוֹת בָּאָדָם. הָאוֹמֵר שֶׁלִּי שֶׁלִּי וְשֶׁלְּךָ שֶׁלָּךְ. זוֹ מִדָּה
בֵּינוֹנִית. וְיֵשׁ אוֹמְרִים זוֹ מִדַּת סְדוֹם. שֶׁלָּךְ וְשֶׁלְּךָ שֶׁלִּי
עַם הָאָרֶץ. שֶׁלִּי שֶׁלָּךְ וְשֶׁלְּךָ שֶׁלָּךְ חָסִיד. שֶׁלָּךְ שֶׁלִּי וְשֶׁלִּי
שֶׁלִּי רָשָׁע:

There are four types among people:
The one who says, What is mine is mine and
*   what is yours is yours—he is the average*
*   type (though some call him the Sodom*
*   type);*
The one who says, What is mine is yours and
*   what is yours is mine—he is ignorant;*
The one who says, what is mine is yours and
*   what is yours is yours—he is a saintly type;*
The one who says, What is yours is mine and
*   what is mine is mine—he is wicked.*
[Avot 5:13]

The Sodom type—
the average
Most of us believe that people deserve what they earn, and
that once we have earned a thing, it belongs to us alone.
Yet the rabbis felt that this could become an evil way of
thinking and acting. They identified it as the belief of the
people of Sodom, which was destroyed by God because of

their wickedness. But why did the rabbis feel it fair to say that most of us are like the people of Sodom? Are we really that wicked when it comes to our attitudes toward possessions and sometimes even beliefs?

The answer to this lies in our mutual need for one another and, sometimes, for one another's property. To put this case in its proper sense, the rabbis reminded us to see everything that we own as a kind of loan from God:

רַבִּי אֶלְעָזָר אִישׁ בַּרְתּוֹתָא אוֹמֵר. תֶּן־לוֹ מִשֶּׁלּוֹ. שָׁאַתָּה
וְשֶׁלְּךָ שֶׁלּוֹ.

Rabbi Eleazar of Bertota said, Give unto [God] of what is His, seeing that you and all that you have are His. [Avot 3:8]

The property of the world is meant to be used in the service of God, no matter whose hands it has passed into, no matter who seems to "own" it.

The cave and the world

Simeon ben Yoḥai was forced to flee to a cave to hide from the Romans he had spoken against. In this hiding place, he was joined by his son; and the two of them lived there for twelve years, studying the Torah.

At the end of the twelfth year, Simeon was told that the Roman emperor had died and the decree against the Jews had been lifted. He and his son came out of the cave and into the full light of the sun, prepared to reenter the life of the Jewish community.

As he approached the city of Jerusalem, however, Simeon saw Jewish farmers tending their fields. Immediately he was enraged and in his anger he called out to them, "How dare you occupy yourselves in this wasted way? The decree of the Romans is lifted. We can study the Torah again! Leave your fields and study."

But the farmers laughed at him. "Now is the time for reaping. Later we will study."

Then Simeon called out, "May these fields burn, for the people turn to what is merely a passing need, while they neglect the eternal truths."

And everywhere that Simeon and his son turned their eyes, the fields were at once consumed by flame.

Until a voice came forth saying, "Have you left your cave to destroy my world? Is it not more important to live by Torah than to study it? Go back to your cave and study your ways." [Shab. 33b]

Living in the world

The object of Jewish teaching is not to separate us from the world of reality, the world of sowing and reaping, but to help us learn how best to live in the real world. What had happened to Simeon during his long stay in hiding in the cave can happen to any one of us if we are not on guard against it.

Simeon had lived so long in a certain way that he was convinced it was the only right way to live. He had become so wrapped up in the study of Torah that he had forgotten a prime rule: "Choose life, that you may live." Instead, he had come to believe in study alone.

All of us would probably agree that study is vitally important to living a Jewish life. But we would probably also agree with Ben Zoma, who blessed the people of the community for helping him by preparing his bread and the clothing he wore. We would also agree with the workman who told Rabbi Yohanan, "I am as important as you." On the question of which is more important, study or action, as Jews we refuse to choose either one at the expense of the other.

Seeking a balance

Solomon Ganzfried (1804–1886), a Hungarian rabbi who edited the manual of Jewish law called the *Kitzur Shulhan Aruch*, wrote the following:

> *The good and right path to follow is the middle course to which one should become accustomed. [A person] should only desire the things which are necessary for the body, and it is impossible to live*

THE PLACE OF POSSESSIONS

We recognize that a person has the right to keep what he has earned. But we also know that all good comes from God and that we should not be indifferent to the needs of others. We should not let study take us out of the world; nor should worldly pursuits make us forget about study.

without them; neither should a man be too much occupied with his business, but only enough to obtain things which are required for the immediate needs of life; neither should he be tight-fisted too much, nor should he spend his money freely, but should give charity according to his means, and lend money readily to the poor; and he should not be too jolly and gay, nor sad and melancholy, but should be happy all his days with satisfaction and friendliness. Relating to all other ethical values also, he who chooses the middle course is called a sage.

Seeking a balance in the things we do—trying to find the middle ground—is a skill, almost an art. Like so many Jewish values, it requires us to keep an open mind and to search for truth.

When Simeon and his son closed their minds to the middle ground, they literally saw everything around them engulfed in flames: in modern terms we might say they "saw red." A person who is unwilling to live by the middle ground is really separating himself from the community.

In the preceding unit we spoke of the complex drives within each of us—of the Yetzer Tov and the Yetzer HaRa that fight and work to control our characters. There are similar forces at work within the community—the people of the community themselves.

The people of the community

Like the individual, the community is best when the forces within it are balanced. When the people of a community live in balance, the community becomes a good place in which to live.

So the rabbis taught that the people of a community should feel natural together, and that they should share with one another. But they should also be willing to argue honestly with one another and each should have the right to his own personal possessions. Beautiful homes and beautiful furniture are good, the rabbis said, because they help to put us "into a cheerful frame of mind" [Ber. 57b]. And that cheerful frame of mind helps the community to be more cheerful, too. But a beautiful home and furniture are of no use if their owner is unhappy with them. So the

Furnishing a home means work; so does keeping it up. But we like to have cheerful surroundings and to open our home to friends. We each possess our own opinions, too. Sometimes we share our opinions with others, but then sometimes we argue. Arguments can be a source of strength for us.

rabbis taught that the true definition of a rich man is "one who finds pleasure through his wealth" [Shab. 25b].

Finding the middle ground

Finding the middle ground in the community is not so very different from seeking a balance within oneself. The first step is finding the extremes, just as we would locate the middle of a rectangle by first locating its four corners.

Four attitudes

The rabbis defined four basic, extreme attitudes toward possessions. There are those who believe that things belong only to the person who owns them, those who believe that things belong to whoever takes them, those who believe that people can't really own anything at all, and those who believe that all things are their own to use. The rabbis expressed these attitudes in the words quoted at the beginning of this chapter.

The wicked type

When a person says, "What is yours is mine and what is mine is mine," he is thinking like a thief. This person would be quite willing to come over to your house, borrow your tennis racket without asking, and then keep it. On the other hand, if you were to ask to borrow a nickel from him, he would be unwilling to make the loan.

The basic characteristic of this type of person is selfishness. His is a case of the Yetzer HaRa in full command, while the real person—the person who might result from a proper balance between the two kinds of Yetzer—is lost.

Such people look out only for themselves and ignore the needs of others. The consequences for the community at large can be disastrous.

The story is told of a king who loved to collect taxes. Year after year, his storehouses were filled to overflowing with gold, silver, and precious gems. Finally, the people of the kingdom had no more money to pay taxes. So the king turned to collecting taxes in payments of wheat or barley, of rice or oats; or in payments of merchandise or goods.

It happened once that a drought lingered in the land and the people grew no crops. Still, the king's tax collectors demanded payment for the king. The people of community met together.

"What can we do?" they asked one another. "Who will go to the king to plead for us?" But all were afraid except one old man.

"I am too old to fear death," the old man said.

The old man came to the palace gates and called out, "I bear a message from the people to the king." And when he was taken to the king, he said, "Your majesty, the people are starving from lack of food and dying of thirst from the drought. You have taken everything from them in taxes, but you have given them nothing in return. Now you must help your people if the kingdom is to survive."

"This is the message my people have sent? Instead I will add new taxes."

"Your majesty," the old man said, "all my life I have been a fisherman on the king's lake. Now I am near death. Would the king grant me a small favor? Come with me in my boat that all may see that I am the king's friend."

"To this I agree," said the king. "For it is a pleasant day and a good time to go boating on my lake."

The old man rowed and the king sat in the bow of the boat. Soon they were in the center of the lake. Then the old man took a drill and began to drill a hole through the bottom of the boat.

"Why are you doing that?" the king asked. "We shall be drowned."

"I am boring the hole only beneath my seat," the fisherman replied. "You have nothing to worry about."

The king stared at the fisherman. Finally he said, "You may put the drill down now. I think I understand. We are in this boat together, just as we are in the world together. And my selfishness has bored a hole in my kingdom. Come, row me back to shore so that I may fix the hole before my whole kingdom is lost." [based on Lev. R. 4:6]

Selfishness removes us from the community, leaving us friendless and alone in the end. It is one corner (an extreme one) of behavior toward others.

The ignorant one   Another extreme is the person who does not understand how society operates at all. The person who says, "What is mine is yours and what is yours is mine" is simply ignorant. This kind of person belongs in a topsy-turvy society in which everything is backward. This person might say, for example, "Here is my new shirt. You wear it." Or, "I like your new blouse. Let me have it."

But the worst thing about this kind of ignorance is that it often causes jealousy. You probably know someone who has a lot of nice things of his own but who still wants the things you have, who always wants to "trade." From time to time, we all seem to want to do that. But when a person carries the desire to "trade" possessions to an extreme, forever thinking of trading things (but mostly others' things), he has developed a jealous eye, which can hardly ever be satisfied. He is at the second of the four corners (extremes).

The saint   Just as the ignorant man's jealousy and the wicked man's greed are harmful to the community, so too is the extreme of acting the part of a saint. When a person says, "What is mine is yours and what is yours is yours"—and acts according to his belief—he becomes a burden for the whole community.

In the time of the Talmud there was one rabbi who gave so freely to charity that the collectors of charity would avoid him. When they saw him coming, they would run the other way. The danger he represented was just the opposite of that of the greedy king: he was apt to give away everything, and so become a beggar himself!

Some religions encourage this kind of action. Many eastern religions teach that a person should give away everything to separate himself from the world and its evil impulses. But the rabbis taught that giving away everything does not help the world at all—in fact, in a way it is selfish, just as selfish as being greedy. For it is just another kind of greed—a greed for holiness, a greed for being a saint.

The person who says, "What is mine is mine and what is yours is yours," is the person who understands that the best society exists when all its members are allowed the freedom to own things and to live without fear of being robbed or cheated. This, the majority of the rabbis said, is the "average" type. Most of us believe this, too.

The average type

But some of the rabbis remind us that this attitude can also be an extreme—one that even threatens the community. If we act according to this attitude slavishly, we forget our neighbor's needs, the needs of the orphan, the widow, and the stranger. This, some of the rabbis pointed out, was the attitude of the people of Sodom, whose city was destroyed by God because of their evil ways.

The Sodom type When we adopt the "average" attitude as our *only* attitude, we are indeed behaving like the people of Sodom.

> *The attitude of the people of Sodom was that each person must keep what belongs to him and not ever share with anyone. When a stranger came to town, they would take gold, silver and jewelry from the town treasury and give it to the stranger. But when the stranger began to complain of hunger, and begged for food for his stomach, the Sodomites refused to give him anything. When the person died of hunger, the jewels and money would be returned to the city treasury and used to tempt other strangers. [Sanh. 109b] [Pirke deR. Eliezer 25]*

> *Once the people of Sodom put a girl to death for sharing. Two girls were at a well drawing water. Said one to the other, "Why are you so pale?"*
>
> *"We have no more food and are ready to die," replied the second girl.*
>
> *What did the first girl do? She filled her pitcher with flour instead of water and they exchanged pitchers, each taking the other's.*
>
> *But when the Sodomites discovered this sharing, they burnt the first girl to death, for the law of the land strictly forbade anyone to give charity. [Gen. R. 49:6]*

Just as the saintly type is an extreme, so the average type can become an extreme too. Charity is necessary for the survival of a society. And we must all agree that sometimes what seems to be "mine" can become rightfully "yours."

Reflection By defining the four types of attitudes toward possessions, the rabbis were showing us the four corners of human behavior. Most of us are somewhere in between these extremes. We may sometimes give charity and at other times be selfish. We may sometimes act wickedly, seeing everything as our own, taking whatever we can by force; and at other times we may act jealously, desiring to have whatever others own and not caring at all for what we already have.

Because the rabbis' concern was with building a good community, a society in which all people are respected and

FOUR TYPES—FOUR CONCERNS OF BEHAVIOR

The rabbis recognized that people hold four different types of attitudes toward property: the average recognizes property rights; the selfish grabs all he can; the ignorant is confused; the saint tends to give too much away. The last three are extremes. The average can become an extreme by never, never sharing.

allowed freedom, they taught that we must take a stand somewhere between the extremes. The attitude that seems most acceptable is that of the "average" type, who says, "What is mine is mine and what is yours is yours." But even this attitude can be harmful to the community if it becomes extreme, if it is followed without any exceptions whatsoever.

As with most matters, the rabbis prefer us to seek a balance—perhaps closer to the positions of the saint and of the average man, but nevertheless a balance of all four. Even jealousy and greed can be turned to good if we work at it—in the same way that the Yetzer HaRa can be used for worthwhile purposes.

Basic to our whole discussion is the idea that we should all agree on what is "mine" and what is "yours." This is the reason for the laws that describe how a person owns a thing and how a person loses a thing, as well as for the Jewish laws that regulate how much charity a person should give and when a person should keep money for family and self.

For such laws to work, they must treat all members of the community equally and the people who administer the laws must be fair.

14

The value of government

רַבִּי חֲנִינָא סְגַן הַכֹּהֲנִים אוֹמֵר. הֱוֵי מִתְפַּלֵּל בִּשְׁלוֹמָהּ שֶׁל
מַלְכוּת. שֶׁאִלְמָלֵא מוֹרָאָהּ אִישׁ אֶת־רֵעֵהוּ חַיִּים בְּלָעוֹ:

*Rabbi Ḥanina said, Pray for the welfare of the
government, since but for the fear of it, people
would swallow each other alive. [Avot 3:2]*

**The importance
of government**

The system of laws under which a people live reflects the
group values of those people. Even something as minor as
a stop sign or a signal at a railroad crossing reflects a basic
value—in each of these cases, the value of protecting the
safety of the members of society. By putting up the stop
sign and the railroad crossing signal, we place into action
our concern for our own safety, the safety of our loved
ones, and the safety of others. Putting values into action is
an important function of government, certainly a function
that makes government desirable.

The best way for us to understand governments in terms

of what we know about individuals is to consider again the whole question of the Yetzer HaRa and the Yetzer Tov. It is one thing for the Torah to teach us, "Do not hate your neighbor in your heart" [Lev. 19:17]. But it is quite another thing to prevent people from hurting others in actuality. The Ten Commandments have been in existence for thousands of years, and still the daily newspapers are filled with reports of murder and robbery, of people who have sworn falsely in courts, of one person cheating another. The plain fact is that while some of us work at controlling our Yetzer HaRa and turning it to useful purposes, others do not. They allow the Yetzer HaRa within them to run wild. Like drunken drivers, then, they become dangerous to everyone else on the road.

Governments are formed to protect us from such people. Just as we must learn to rule our Yetzer HaRa on an individual level, an important purpose of government is to control those on the group level whose Yetzer HaRa has gone wild.

Law enforcement and courts

In order for a government to effectively protect us, each of us must give up some of his own free will. There are constantly great disputes and debates over how much power should be given to the government. But we can see without any dispute that everyone must give up *some* power if the government is to be effective in protecting us.

A good example of this is our giving up as individuals our right to revenge. Revenge is destructive to the group. Suppose A steals from B, and then B steals in return from A, saying that now things are even. If this were the end of it, all might be fine—although revenge is seldom any fairer than the original injustice. But when B takes revenge, he may take a little more from A than A took from him. Then A himself feels the need for revenge. Soon, things get out of hand, and A and B are at the point of killing each other —their friends and relatives may get into the act, too.

To avoid this kind of situation we allow government the power to provide law enforcement in the form of police and other agencies, as well as courts of law in which cases may be heard and settled. Law enforcement agencies and courts of law both represent powers that are best held by the group rather than by the individual, for the sake of us all.

"An eye for an eye" The Talmud may be seen partly as the records of an ongoing court of law in which the rabbis tried case after case to establish the boundaries of government. As in our example, the classic case of revenge treated by the Talmud centers around the biblical formula demanding "an eye for an eye and a tooth for a tooth." To see how the "government" (in this case, the rabbis of the Talmud) sought to control the group Yetzer HaRa, consider the following discussion:

> "Eye for eye"—that means a payment of money.
> You say that it means a payment of money; but perhaps it really means that an actual eye must be forfeited!
> Supposing, however, that the eye of the one was large and of the other small, how can I in that case apply the law "eye for eye"?
> . . . Or supposing a blind man had knocked out the eye of another, or a lame man had made another lame, how can I fulfill in these cases "eye for eye"? The Torah demands, "You shall have one manner of law" (Lev. 24:22)—that means a law which shall be the same for all of you. [Baba K. 83b]

The law must always treat all persons as equals because our basic value is that all are created equal by God. But if this is the case, the rabbis argued, "an eye for an eye" can only mean that if a person should put out the eye of another, the guilty one must pay a sum of money to compensate for the eye he has destroyed.

In this way, the government steps in to interpret the law to the benefit of all members of society. It does no real good to the person who has lost an eye or a limb if the one who injured him loses an eye or a limb in return. The monetary payment, while it cannot replace the original eye or limb, can at least help in some way to make up for the pain and loss that occur when a person is injured.

ENFORCING THE LAW

If all obeyed the Torah, there would be no need for policemen and law courts. But since many are carried away by the Yetzer HaRa, police must keep order and arrest offenders. Judges must hear cases and pass sentence. We have given up our private rights of vengeance to our government. Blood feuds have given place to more orderly procedures.

The rabbis looked forward to the day when each person would rule himself according to the laws of God. If all of us were to follow the principle of Hillel—"Do not to others what is hateful to yourself"—there would be no need for governments and rulers to control society. Each of us would be a government in miniature, successfully controlling our Yetzer HaRa and concentrating on doing what is good.

The perfect government

Thus the rabbis dreamed of the End of Days, when each man and woman would grow so much in wisdom and in the fear of Heaven that there would be no need for governments. But though they could be dreamers and while they planned for a world that would be ruled by God alone, the rabbis were realistic, too. They realized that people are still not in control of their own evil impulses. So they recognized the need for common government, "since but for the fear of it, people would swallow each other alive."

The phrase "swallow each other alive" may seem very harsh. But it is a realistic picture of what happens when governments do not work. We think of the American West of the nineteenth century as the "Wild West" because law and order were kept in the same way that they were broken. Lawmen acted in precisely the same manner as the outlaws they opposed. The government was usually the result of the stronger killing the weaker.

The evils of government

The rabbis dreamed of a day when there would be no further need for government because they were aware of the fact that governments "swallow up" the very citizens they are supposed to protect. That is, governments have a way of growing in power and taking away more and more freedom from the people being governed.

The evils of authoritarian government were being pointed out to the Jewish people as far back as the time of the Prophet Samuel. The people came to Samuel and demanded that he appoint a king to rule over them, so that they could be like all the other nations of their time.

> *The thing displeased Samuel when they said: "Give us a king to judge us." And Samuel prayed to the Lord.*
>
> *But the Lord said to Samuel: "Listen to the voice of the people in all that they say to you; for they have not rejected you, but they have rejected Me, that I should not be king over them."* [1 Sam. 8:6–7]

Samuel then warned the people of the dangers of allowing a king to rule over them:

> *This will be the custom of the king who will reign over you: he will take your sons and appoint them for himself, for his chariots, and to be his horsemen; and they shall run before his chariots. And he will appoint them for himself as captains of thousands, and of fifties; and to plow his ground, and to reap his harvest, and to make instruments for war, and the instruments for his chariots. And he will take your daughters to be perfumers, and to be cooks, and to be bakers. And he will take your fields, and your vineyards, and your oliveyards, even the best of them, and give them to his servants. . . .*
>
> *And you shall cry out in that day because of your king whom you shall have chosen for yourself; and the Lord will not answer you in that day.* [1 Sam. 8:11–14, 18]

This is the classic Jewish warning against the power of kings and overblown governments. Whenever we give up our rights and form a government instead of learning to govern ourselves, the government gains power over us.

In the time of the Bible, the king was controlled somewhat by the Torah itself. When a new king rose over Israel, his first duty was to copy out an entire Sefer Torah in his own handwriting so that he could not later claim that he did not know the law.

In the United States, our government is controlled by the Constitution, and our basic rights are protected by the first ten amendments to the Constitution, called the Bill of Rights. Here are guarantees to each person of freedom of worship, of speech, of the press, of assembly, and of petition to the government. Further guarantees include the right to bear arms, freedom from having to provide quar-

GIVE US A KING?

We have not yet reached the point where there is no need of government. But the rabbis knew that government itself could become a threat to its citizens. The people of Israel demanded a king so that they could be like the other nations around them. But Samuel knew what the price of kingship could be.

ters for soldiers, from unreasonable searches and seizures, from being detained without being charged for a crime, from being tried twice for the same crime, from having to testify against oneself, and from being "deprived of life, liberty or property without due process of law." The Bill of Rights also safeguards our rights to a speedy and public trial by an impartial jury and prohibits excessive bails and fines and "cruel and unusual punishment."

We began this chapter by saying that a system of law reflects the values of a people. In the case of the Bill of Rights, those values are openly expressed in an earlier document, the Declaration of Independence, adopted July 4, 1776, by the Second Continental Congress.

> We hold these truths to be self-evident, that all men are created equal, that they are endowed by their Creator with certain unalienable Rights, that among these are Life, Liberty and the pursuit of Happiness—that to secure these rights, Governments are instituted among Men, deriving their just powers from the consent of the governed.

This is a brief but forceful statement of the position of a government and of the people that created it.

All are created equal The Declaration of Independence begins by declaring it self-evident that "all men are created equal." Yet it was not always self-evident. In ancient Egypt, no commoner thought of himself or herself as equal to the pharaoh. The pharaoh was considered a god-man, separate and above all other people. No one else was equal to the pharaoh.

On the other hand, even when the Kingdom of Israel was at its greatest strength and the king most powerful, the king was never confused with God. The Prophet Nathan felt free to rebuke King David for the wrongs the king had committed in stealing another man's wife and sending that man to his death in battle. And in reply, David, far from answering, "I am the king and I shall do as I please," instead prayed for forgiveness from God.

The difference between the pharaoh and the king of

Israel was that the Jewish people had been taught the equality of all men.

> *Why was man created singly? Why did God create only one man? So that no one can boast, "I am of nobler lineage," our Sages explain. All mankind is descended from the same man. All are equal before God. [Sanh. 38a]*

It is this teaching of the rabbis to which the men of the Second Continental Congress were referring when they declared "all men are created equal" to be a truth that is self-evident. It is self-evident only when we remember that no man is closer to God than another.

Unalienable rights

Neither are our rights to life, liberty, and the pursuit of happiness simply values that we have dreamed up for ourselves. Even according to the Declaration of Independence upon which many of our country's civil laws are based, our rights are derived from our Creator, the Lord God.

No person has the right to say to another, "I forbid you to live"—which is exactly what the murderer says to his victim. God has ruled, "You shall not murder."

No person has the right to say to another, "I forbid you to be free—which is exactly what the master tells the slave. God has ruled, "You shall be free."

And no person, whether by swearing falsely in a court of law, or by stealing, or by injuring his neighbor, can forbid another to pursue his own happiness. For all of these actions are forbidden by the Lord, and the right to the pursuit of happiness is guaranteed by the Law of Heaven, the commandments of God.

To secure these rights

We can now understand the reasoning of the men of the Second Continental Congress, as well as that of the Men of the Great Assembly in ancient times, in declaring a need for government among people. That need is to secure and safeguard the rights that are the inheritance of all who are born human—of all who are created in the image of God.

In order to insure our freedom, we establish a government with the power to limit and safeguard our freedom. In order to protect ourselves from the government, we in turn establish laws of protection for the people. The power of government, then, should never be allowed to become greater than the power of the values that government is supposed to protect.

Where does the power of government come from? It comes from us, from "the people." But as we have seen, government has the tendency to overreach itself and grow larger and more powerful.

LAW ABOVE ALL

The powers of the king of Israel were limited by the
Torah; the powers of our federal government are
limited by the Constitution, especially by the Bill
of Rights. The Declaration of Independence states
that all men are created equal. The power of
government comes first from the people and
ultimately from God.

Where does the power of the values behind the government come from? This power is an endowment from God,
the Creator. "All men are created equal, . . . endowed by
their Creator with certain unalienable rights."

Government and power Thus we have seen that there is a tension between the need for government and the need to distrust government. We need government to keep us from "swallowing up" one another. But we need instruments such as the Bill of Rights and the Talmud to protect us from the government!

Often, no matter what it is doing, a government claims it is doing only what is good. "What is good" may mean putting to death "enemies of the government," overtaxing citizens, or waging war. No wonder Rabban Gamaliel warned us:

הֱווּ זְהִירִין בָּרָשׁוּת. שֶׁאֵין מְקָרְבִין לוֹ לְאָדָם אֶלָּא לְצֹרֶךְ
עַצְמָן. נִרְאִין כְּאוֹהֲבִין בִּשְׁעַת הֲנָאָתָן. וְאֵין עוֹמְדִין לוֹ
לְאָדָם בִּשְׁעַת דָּחֲקוֹ:

Be mindful of the ruling powers, for they bring no one near them save for their own need; they seem to be friends at such time as it is to their own gain, but they stand not by a person when he is in distress. [Avot 2:3]

We cannot truly make friends with power.

Consider a typical political election. Before the election, all the candidates make promises to the voters. They are friendly and cheerful toward everyone who calls upon them. They listen to complaints and promise to try to correct things and make them better. After all, they need our votes. But as soon as the election is over, promises are all too often forgotten. Especially in times of crisis, when pressures mount on all sides, government officials act not so much in the interests of the people as of the government itself.

Perhaps that is why one of the Psalms says, "Do not put your trust in princes, . . . for in them there is no help" [Psalms 146:3].

Nahmias, a fourteenth-century commentator, told the following parable about the friendship of the powerful:

A king once promoted one of his officers. Each day the king would rise up before this officer and kiss him on the neck. In the end the king slew him and said that he used to kiss the spot where the sword would land when the officer's head was cut off. Folks say: Do not think the lion is smiling when he bares his teeth; it is only to devour. Human kings are too often like the lions of the animal kingdom.

The warning of Samuel, the parable of Nahmias, and the warning of Gamaliel concern the way of all governments. No government may be totally trusted. We must constantly watch the progress of power.

The law of the land Even so, the Talmudic dictum is that "The law of the land is law" [Baba K. 113a]. And the rabbis ruled, "A person must respect the government" [Mechilta, Bo].

Here, too, we must balance our interpretation. The law of the land is *not* always law. Even the rabbis had to defy the law of Rome when Hadrian forbade the study of Torah and the practice of Judaism. When the law of the land comes into conflict with the higher law of God—from which all governments gain their right to rule—the law of God is the law that must be followed.

Creating a dream Our dream is of a world ruled according to the laws of the Torah, the laws of compassion and kindness, of justice and mercy, of consideration and respect. But to make such a dream a reality, we must become a "light unto the nations." If the Jews are the "chosen" people, it is because we bear the message of Torah to all.

> *The Torah was given publicly and openly in a place to which no one had any claim. For if it had been given in the Land of Israel, the nations of the world could have said, "We have no portion in this." Therefore it was given in the wilderness, publicly and openly, and in a place to which no one had any claim. Everyone who desires to accept it, let him come and accept it. [Mechilta, Bahodesh, Yitro]*

The task is great and we cannot even hope to complete it. Yet we must each of us feel responsible for bringing the laws of God into our world—for teaching the Torah and acting according to the commandments. Not only should we not separate ourselves from the community, we must participate in it as much as possible and help make its laws conform more and more to the laws of the Torah. Then there will be no problem and nothing to fear when we follow the dictum of the Talmud—"The law of the land is law" [Baba K. 113a].

**The governments of nations can present great
problems: disregard for the individual, doing wrong
in the name of good, hypocrisy, broken promises.
Hope for the future lies in bringing the law of
Torah into the world so that the world may someday
know the reign of justice and compassion.**

Reflection

The rabbis recognized two opposing forces in our need for government—lest men "swallow each other alive"—and our need to cautiously watch the progress of power while keeping alive the dream of a time when governments will bow before the rule of God.

Our values are reflected in the kinds of laws we pass and obey. Working for the coming of God's rule on earth, therefore, means not separating ourselves from the community. It means working in the community to create an acceptance for the laws of Torah. It means striving to make the laws of the land reflect the values of Jewish teachings.

The value of government   157

OUR COUNTRY, right or wrong. When right, to be kept right; when wrong, to be put right.

We are required as Jews to involve ourselves in the world. We must take a stand and fight when we feel that something is wrong with government. We must learn, too, to work within the system of laws under which we live in order to change and alter them and bring them into line with what we believe. In short, we must "pray for the welfare of the government," while adopting a responsible attitude, the attitude of a good citizen.

> *Rabbi Oshaya taught: In human practice, when a mortal king builds a palace, he builds it not with his own skill, but with the skills of an architect. The architect moreover does not build it out of his own head, but employs plans and diagrams to know how to arrange the chambers and doors.*
> *Thus God consulted the Torah and then created the world.*
> *[Gen. R. 1:1]*

So, too, if we wish to know how the world can best be governed, we should consult the architect's plans for the building of a righteous world—the laws of the Torah. In truth, there can be no better government than that upon which the entire world is based—the government of God alone.

15

The value of judging

אַל תָּדִין אֶת־חֲבֵרְךָ עַד שֶׁתַּגִּיעַ לִמְקוֹמוֹ.

Hillel said, Judge not your companion until you have been in his place. [Avot 2:5]

One of Judaism's central values is the justice which results of wise judgment. What makes justice and judgment so important is the large part that they play in your daily life. You are a judge of others. You judge how others should act. You ask yourself, "Is this person being faithful to me?" and you make a judgment by answering yes or no. You ask, "Is this person a good and honest neighbor, or is he a cheat and a liar?" and you judge by deciding one way or another. You ask, "Is this person being fair to me?" and answer by judging yes or no.

Although you do not wear the robes of a courtroom judge as you decide the cases that come before you day by day, you do hold a kind of mental court. From friends you expect and demand one kind of action and from enemies a far different kind. You expect teachers to be fair, policemen to be hōnest, rabbis to be good, clowns to be cheerful,

relatives to be generous, mailmen to be dependable, doctors to be concerned, and lawyers to be on your side. Both when people act as you expect them to and when they do not, you pass judgment.

And as you judge, a strange thing happens: you begin to define yourself, to find out just where you belong. For each judgment that you make is on the basis of what you know and what you learn, the evidence that you gather. If you generally expect others to be fair, you will begin to regard fairness as a value in which you believe. When you expect others to be honest, you begin to value honesty for yourself. Of course, the same is true the other way around, too. When you judge others unfairly, you begin to forget fairness for yourself also; and when you are dishonest in your judgment of those around you, you soon begin to lie to yourself as well.

Judging honestly is a skill that we learn. We are not automatically born with the ability of judging well. In learning to judge, we must learn to gather all the evidence, sift it, choose our values, and then make a decision based on our choices.

So it is obvious that Hillel's saying, which forms the theme for this chapter:

> Judge not your companion until you have been in his place.
> [Avot 2:5]

is addressed to the way in which you judge the people around you every day.

In his place Judging becomes very complex when we put ourselves in the "place" of another person, when we try to see things the way they see them. Yet judging can be fair only if we do this. In a way, it is a part of the process of gathering evidence, and it is what Joshua ben Perahyah had in mind when he said, "Judge all people favorably" [Avot 1:6]. It is a question of judging as we wish ourselves to be judged.

After all, we want other people to see us in the best possible way, especially when something we do does not come out right. Being human involves making mistakes and learning and growing through the mistakes we make. When every one of our mistakes is judged harshly, we begin to worry so much about not making mistakes that we are stunted in our growth.

So it is best when we judge other people favorably, when we are willing to give others a "second chance" or "the benefit of the doubt." This, after all, is what we hope others will do in judging our own actions.

More than that, we hope that before people make judgments about what we have done, they give us a chance to explain. This involves the process of gathering evidence before making a decision. In trying to place ourselves in someone else's shoes, we have to try to gather all the possible evidence to understand why that person acted in the way he did.

Gathering evidence

The rabbis told a story about how misleading judgment can be when it is not based on solid evidence, when we jump to a conclusion before all the facts are in:

Rav Ashi was once teaching a lesson in the Mishnah and came to the story of the Jewish king, Manasseh. Manasseh, he explained to the students, had turned to idolatry. As he began to explain the times in which Manasseh lived, however, the class time was over.

"Tomorrow," he said in closing, "we will speak further of this 'wise' man."

Now the Tradition tells us that Manasseh was truly a wise man, but Ashi said the word "wise" with a tone of sarcasm, as if to say that Manasseh was really ignorant.

That night, in a dream, Manasseh came to Rav Ashi.

"Do you honestly judge me to be ignorant?" Manasseh asked. Then the king asked Ashi some difficult questions of Jewish law and when Ashi could not reply, Manasseh answered the questions brilliantly, amazing the learned scholar.

With humility, Rav Ashi asked the ancient king of Judah, "If you were so learned, how did you come to worship idols?"

Manasseh replied, "Had you been there with me, you would have gathered up the hem of your garment and run after me to worship idols!" [Sanh. 102b]

RIGHTEOUS JUDGMENT

To judge rightly we must know for sure that a person has done wrong. (We can't go by hearsay or circumstantial evidence.) Even then, we must put ourselves in the place of the accused. In what circumstances was the wrong committed? What pressures may have been brought to bear on him?

Ashi's error was a common one: He was willing to pass judgment without really trying to imagine himself in Manasseh's place. This is what happens when we do not gather the facts before we judge. If, for example, you hear a rumor that so and so did such and such and you judge that person without asking if what you heard is the truth or without trying to understand why that person might have acted in such a way, you are repeating Rav Ashi's error. Rabbi Ishmael used to say, "He who lays down decisions without knowing all the facts is foolish, wicked and arrogant" [Avot 4:9]. So Ashi learned.

Balancing justice

Truly understanding the actions of another, truly imagining yourself in his place, requires sympathy and mercy. Ben Azzai said this in a slightly different way:

אַל תְּהִי בָז לְכָל אָדָם. וְאַל תְּהִי מַפְלִיג לְכָל דָּבָר. שֶׁאֵין לְךָ אָדָם שֶׁאֵין לוֹ שָׁעָה. וְאֵין לְךָ דָבָר שֶׁאֵין לוֹ מָקוֹם:

Despise no person, and deem nothing impossible, for there is no one who has not his hour, and there is no thing which has not its place. [Avot 4:3]

To do a person justice, we must be willing to "walk a mile" in his shoes, to learn the things that trouble him, to be compassionate and sympathetic.

Justice and mercy, then, are two sides of the same coin. Society survives best and remains most fair when both are in operation. Either by itself will spoil the community, but the two together help bring about peace.

Much of Pirke Avot is concerned with the way in which judges should act. But the study of judging is not meant only for people who are about to become lawyers and judges. It is meant for all of us to understand better how to judge our neighbors carefully, how we can be just and merciful in the same act of judging, and how our community can be built in the image of God, who is both Truthful Judge and All-Merciful.

The poor and rich alike

In judging, we should not consider someone better or worse because he is rich, better or worse because he is poor. When it comes to making a judgment, people should be treated on the basis of the law alone—they should be treated as total equals before the law. We are even warned that neither party in a case should stand while the other sits, just so that there will be no apparent difference between them.

Once a poor man borrowed a sum of money from a wealthy merchant, promising to repay the loan at the end of two weeks. Two weeks passed, and still another two weeks, but the beggar did not repay his debt. To the rich man it was a small sum; but to the beggar who could not raise it, it was a great deal indeed.

At last the wealthy merchant came down to where the poor man lived and knocked harshly on the door. "Have you my money to return?" he asked. But the poor man answered, "No."

"In that case," said the rich man, "You must come with me before the court and the judge will decide what shall be done with you."

At once the townspeople knew what had happened—for gossip in a small town is like water in a sponge, in an instant every space is filled with it. As the rich man pulled the poor man toward the courtroom, the whole town gathered to march behind the dismal duo.

"Come and judge a case of law," the wealthy merchant called out to the judge. So the judge donned his black hat and robe and sat behind his table.

The courtroom was full of townspeople. Everyone listened as the merchant told of the loan and the broken agreement. Then they heard the beggar tell of how he had been unable to raise enough money to repay his debt.

Suddenly the courtroom was alive with whispers. "The merchant does not need this money." "He has enough money without it." "It is such a small amount that he will not miss it at all." "Why does he not forget the money and count it as charity?"

But the judge called out, "Silence!" and a hush spread over the crowded room.

"Now I will pronounce the verdict," said the judge. "This beggar must return the money he owes immediately. That is justice; and that is what justice requires."

The people were dismayed. But before they could begin to whisper again, the judge stood up. Taking off his black judge's hat, he turned it upside down. "Now," he said, "I will collect charity from you people.

TEMPERING JUSTICE WITH MERCY

As God is both just and merciful, so man, in His image and likeness, should also temper justice with mercy. The judge in our story doubtless knew that the people in the courtroom wished mercy to be shown to the accused. Was it not right that they do their part in making that mercy possible?

Reach into your pockets and help this poor man pay what he owes our rich neighbor. That is mercy; and that is what mercy requires."

It is the combination of justice and mercy that makes the cold reality of the law into the warm life of the good society. And it has always been so.

The result of combining justice and mercy is peace. When we judge others fairly and consider them in the light of mercy, we bring people who are in disagreement back to a position of peace. Disagreement uncontrolled is destructive, whereas peace is basically creative. Therefore, the rabbis said:

The result of justice and mercy

> *For every judge who judges truly, even for an hour, it is counted as if he had been a partner with God in the work of creation.*
> *[Shab. 10a]*

When the person who is judging turns justice into personal power, the work of judging becomes destructive. But when it is done fairly, combining justice and mercy, the task of judging becomes creative, bringing order to the community and binding it together.

Guarding justice Most destructive of all is a person who accepts a bribe in judging and then perverts justice. Even the hint of a bribe is so divisive to a community that the rabbis, following the law of the Torah, forbade it and promised punishment for it. Even a helping hand could be enough of a bribe to disqualify a person from judging a case legally.

> *Once Rabbi Samuel was getting on to a ferry boat: A man came and gave him a helping hand. When Samuel asked why the man happened to be there, the man replied, "I have a lawsuit." Then Samuel said, "I am forbidden to be your judge."* [Ket. 105b]

Injustice spoils the happiness of the community. When even one judge is found to be guilty of accepting a bribe, people come to suspect all judges, and the laws that make for peace between people become useless words printed on paper with no meaning in reality. Therefore, the rabbis' qualifications for a judge were very strict.

A judge must be "wise, humble, sin-fearing, of good repute, and popular with his neighbors" [Tosefta, Sanh. 7:1]. And although these requirements seem great, they can hardly be great enough, for the judge is called upon to act in the name of God and to decide cases involving God's laws and God's children. Therefore, a person "who appoints an unfit judge is as though he had set up an idol in the midst of Israel" [Sanh. 7b]. As Rabbi Eleazar said, "The whole Torah rests upon justice" [Exod. R. 30:19].

Sifting the evidence Even once the evidence is in, the task of judging is not easy. Facts sometimes do lie, or may prove misleading. The truth is not always what it seems to be, and we must learn to sift the evidence carefully, examining all the witnesses and the facts thoroughly before accepting them. Many a good detective story begins with all the evidence pointing to one person as the murderer, but as the story progresses we find that someone else entirely is the guilty one.

The rabbis recorded one such case to warn us of the importance of sifting the evidence before accepting it:

> The witnesses testified, "We saw the accused person run after a man with a sword in his hand. The victim entered a shop as he was fleeing, and the accused murderer ran in after him. When we came into the shop, we found the victim dead on the floor. In the accused man's hand was the sword, still dripping blood."
>
> Yet the murderer was acquitted because the witnesses had not seen the murder take place and so they could not be absolutely positive that the accused man had actually committed the crime. [Tosefta, Sanh. 7:3]

Even the slightest amount of doubt, the slightest lack of evidence, should be weighed in favor of a person who is accused.

We often forget this in our everyday lives. We hear a story about someone, believe it, and pass it on without ever bothering to find out whether it is the truth. The rabbis called this practice the "third tongue," and also Lashon HaRa, the "Evil Tongue." Today we call it slander. The law advises us never to bear a tale from one person to another, even if it seems to be the complete truth—and even when the person we are talking about is present!

Religious awareness and mercy

Being kind in judgment is usually a case of drawing upon our religious awareness. It calls for creativity, for thoughtfulness and imagination. Justice without mercy can be a very grim thing indeed. It is mercy and sympathy that make life bearable.

The judge who took off his hat and collected charity from those who were concerned for mercy was using his religious awareness to create peace in a dispute. We, too, are blessed with the ability to find solutions that are not only just but also merciful. But to do so, we must use our imagination.

Mercy requires that once we have judged fairly, we set aside our judging and forget the evil that has been done. A person who has accepted judgment, who has paid the fine for what he has done, who has served his sentence in jail, or who has agreed to make good what was destroyed should no longer be considered guilty. Once the verdict is given and accepted, and the punishment over, we should strive to see the guilty person as innocent again.

יְהוּדָה בֶן־טַבַּי אוֹמֵר. אַל תַּעַשׂ עַצְמְךָ כְּעוֹרְכֵי הַדַּיָּנִים. וּכְשֶׁיִּהְיוּ בַּעֲלֵי הַדִּין עוֹמְדִים לְפָנֶיךָ יִהְיוּ בְעֵינֶיךָ כִּרְשָׁעִים. וּכְשֶׁנִּפְטָרִים מִלְּפָנֶיךָ יִהְיוּ בְעֵינֶיךָ כְזַכָּאִים. כְּשֶׁקִּבְּלוּ עֲלֵיהֶם אֶת־הַדִּין:

Judah ben Tabbai said, When the [two parties in a case] stand before you, see them both as wicked; and when they have departed your presence, see them both as innocent, the verdict having been accepted by them. [Avot 1:8]

Reflection This attitude works on another level, too. If someone apologizes to you for some wrong he has committed against you, you must use your religious awareness to try to see that person fresh and new again—as a friend.

As long as we remember that the purpose of the rule of law is to create peace between neighbors and friends, we can see that justice and mercy must be combined if peace is to be achieved. The most destructive feeling of all is the inner feeling that revenge is best. When we harbor hatred in our hearts, we give rise to the Yetzer HaRa within us. Soon we forget that we are the creation of God and that our neighbor is His creation, too; and we see our enemy as evil. So we are evil in return. To be insulted and not to react by insulting; to be reproached and not to answer; to be peaceful even when you are being oppressed—these are the signs of a person with religious awareness, a person who has balanced justice with mercy, a person who has not forgotten that the best result is the peaceful one.

All of us are judges. We are called upon to judge our

JUSTICE AND BEYOND

Wrong judgment harms not only the accused, but also the whole community by weakening our trust in laws and government. True justice allows for forgiveness when a wrong has been paid for or an apology given. To refuse to retaliate is to go even beyond justice—to hasten the End of Days.

neighbors and friends every day. Much of how we act toward our companions depends on this action of judging; and much of the way in which we see ourselves depends on what we require from others.

The Tradition teaches us that God is the Truthful Judge; and so, too, it calls God the All-Merciful One. If God judged the world in accordance with the strictest justice, the world would deserve destruction for even the slightest turning away from His law. On the other hand, if God ruled the world only in His aspect as the All-Merciful One, the world would soon overflow with evildoers begging forgiveness one moment and turning away to do evil the next. So God balances justice with mercy, as we balance hot water with cold, to create the warmth that is most pleasing [Gen. R. 12:15]. Acting in the image of God means judging not only through the strict rule of law and justice, but by the warmer measure of mercy and kindness. The result of this combination is peace for the community.

Our judgments should also be based on a gathering and sifting of the facts. Until we know about a person's origins, about the kind of life he has had to lead, the kinds of things he has done, and the kinds of things that have been done to him, we should not judge him.

The value of judging 169

A group of rabbis once went to collect charity from a man called Barbuḥin, but as they approached his home, they heard his son ask, "What are we to eat today?"

Barbuḥin replied, "The cheapest vegetables you find in the marketplace."

The rabbis then said to themselves, "Why should we approach this man? Let us first collect charity in the town and afterward we will come to him." For they had little hope of his giving them a large contribution.

But when they returned from the town and said to him, "Give us a contribution," he said, "Go to my wife and she will give you a bushel of coins."

They went to his wife and said to her, "Your husband bids you give us a contribution of a bushel of dinars."

"Did he say a level bushel or one heaped-up?" she asked.

They answered, "He simply said a bushel."

"Well," she said, "I will give it to you heaped-up and if he complains, I will repay him from my own money."

The rabbis, carrying the bushel overflowing with coins, returned to Barbuḥin to thank him.

"Did my wife give you a level bushel or one heaped-up?" he asked.

They replied, "We said to her, 'simply a bushel,' and she gave us one heaped-up, and said that if you complained she would take it of her own money."

He said, "In fact, I wanted it done so. I intended that it be heaped-up. But why did you not come to me in the first place?"

"We heard your son ask what to buy for supper and you answered, 'the cheapest vegetables,' and so we thought you stingy."

Barbuḥin said, "With myself I am stingy, but with the requirements of my Creator I am not." [Esther R. 2:3]

So you see that until all the facts are in, judgment cannot be fair. The cause of peace can be served only when a person withholds judgment until he has gathered all the evidence.

So Rabbi Ishmael ben Yose said:

אַל תְּהִי דָן יְחִידִי. שֶׁאֵין דָּן יְחִידִי אֶלָּא אֶחָד.

Judge not alone, for none may judge alone save [the Lord.]
[Avot 4:10]

16

The value of delight

כֹּל שֶׁרוּחַ הַבְּרִיּוֹת נוֹחָה הֵימֶנּוּ. רוּחַ הַמָּקוֹם נוֹחָה הֵימֶנּוּ. וְכֹל שֶׁאֵין רוּחַ הַבְּרִיּוֹת נוֹחָה הֵימֶנּוּ. אֵין רוּחַ הַמָּקוֹם נוֹחָה הֵימֶנּוּ:

Ḥanina used to say, He in whom the spirit of his companions takes delight, in him the Spirit of the All-Present takes delight; and he in whom the spirit of his companions takes not delight, in him the Spirit of the All-Present takes not delight. [Avot 3:13]

Among our friends, in clubs, in school, and even at parties and dances, we constantly divide ourselves up into smaller groups. Sometimes it seems that some of these groups are more desirable than others. Sometimes we hear that a small group of people have formed a "secret society" restricted to just a few. Sometimes it is just a "clique," a small group of friends who think that they are better or special for some reason.

We all want to be a part of the best group. We want to have friends who are members of the "in" crowd, the group or clique that seems to have the most fun together.

To become a part of the "in" clique, we sometimes do things that we would otherwise not consider doing.

In itself, this desire to be friendly and popular is not bad. But sometimes we let it go to extremes. Sometimes, just to be popular, you might disobey your parents or disregard the instructions of a teacher when normally you would not. But being popular seems so important. You might even hurt others to gain popularity. If the people you wish to be your friends say, "Everyone does it," you might just find yourself doing it, too.

We have all known a boy or a girl who suddenly became popular and then forgot friends made before. As soon as this person becomes a part of the "in" group, he or she wants nothing more to do with "old" friends. When our concept of popularity carries us to such extremes, it is merely evil.

Following the crowd Popularity is a good example of a "value of the marketplace." And like all the values of the marketplace that we have encountered, popularity becomes harmful when we do not learn to balance it.

In the Book of Exodus we read the commandment "You shall not follow a multitude to do evil" [Exod. 23:2]. When we allow our desire to be popular to become too important, we lose our self-identity. We begin to do whatever the people around us are doing, just so that they will accept us. For example, if the group that we wish to join smokes, we may begin to smoke just so that we will not be different. When we do this, our need for popularity has become so great that we have forgotten our individuality. We are smoking only so that the others will be pleased with us.

But the truth of the matter is that once you lose your individuality, there is very little left for others to take delight in. Allowing any single value to capture us completely is a sure way of losing our sense of balance, and with it our sense of what is truly best for us.

Two kinds of love Just being popular is not always worth the price we pay. The desire to be loved by everyone can lead us far afield. It often leads us to being loved by no one at all.

כָּל אַהֲבָה שֶׁהִיא תְלוּיָה בְדָבָר. בָּטֵל דָּבָר בָּטְלָה אַהֲבָה.
וְשֶׁאֵינָהּ תְּלוּיָה בְדָבָר. אֵינָהּ בְּטֵלָה לְעוֹלָם.

Whenever love depends on some material reason, with the passing
away of that reason, the love too passes away; but if it is not
dependent on such a reason, it will last forever. [Avot 5:19]

The rabbis of Pirke Avot, in discussing love and our need
to be loved by others, found that there are two kinds of
love. Since all of our friendships are based on love, we
could say that there are two kinds of friendships—and
even two kinds of popularity.

One kind of friendship is that based upon a selfish
reason. The rabbis called this a "material reason," because
most often it has to do with what we can "buy" or "get"
through making friends with a certain person. If we know,
for example, that Susy Smiley is a popular girl, we may
make friends with her just so that we can be popular, too.
Or we may ignore Sally Plain, even though she wants to be
friendly, simply because she is not popular. We might
want to be the friend of Pete Pitcher because we know that

FALSE FRIENDSHIP

**False friendship is usually based on some ulterior
motive—the hope for material gain, the desire to
"get ahead," the wish to appear popular and
important. False friendship passes away when the
hope for selfish gain is gone.**

he can help get us on the baseball team—and we might ignore Sam Scholar because he doesn't even know how to play baseball.

Of course, if Susy Smiley suddenly becomes unpopular, we tend to forget her quickly. After all, the *only* reason we made friends with her was because of her popularity. And if Pete Pitcher turns out to be a bad baseball player and is dropped from the team, we may forget him in the same way, since he is no longer very useful to us.

It is little wonder that the rabbis said that "with the passing away of [the] reason, the love too passes away." When a friendship is based only on something material, it does not usually grow in strength.

The lasting friendship Lasting friendships may begin through either material causes or through sharing experiences, but in either case they are built on mutual trust and love. The best example of the kind of friendship that bears the test of time is found in the biblical account of David and Jonathan. Jonathan was the son of King Saul. But at one point, Saul warned his son that friendship with David might mean that Jonathan would lose the chance to become the next king of Israel.

> *"So long as David lives upon the earth," Saul warned his son, "neither you nor your kingdom shall be established."*
> [1 Sam. 20:31]

Yet Jonathan, who knew that he might lose the chance to be king by being David's friend, pledged himself to David, saying, "You shall be king over Israel, and I shall be second to you" [1 Sam. 23:17].

The Bible tells us that "the soul of Jonathan was knit with the soul of David, and Jonathan loved him as his own soul" [1 Sam. 18:1].

Just as we do not need to explain why we should be concerned with ourselves, why we should care for ourselves, so too we do not need to explain why we care for our friends. Friendship is the pledge of one soul to another; it is a bond between one person and another, which needs no explanation at all.

TRUE FRIENDSHIP

True friendship needs no reasons. It is based on what the friend is, the qualities we see and value in him or her. True friendship is lasting. And if it requires some sacrifices, the sacrifices are forthcoming.

Still, the case of Jonathan and David was an extreme, too. Although Jonathan's concern for David was heroic, and highly to be praised, still it is obvious that Saul was right —Jonathan did not become the next king. Normally, the rabbis would prefer that we do not forget ourselves, even for the sake of our friends. What makes Jonathan's actions truly praiseworthy is that David was in real danger of his life, and Jonathan was helping to protect him. For the sake of life, one must forget everything else—except one's own life. Thus, Jonathan warned David to flee for his life whether or not it meant that the kingdom would eventually be David's and not Jonathan's.

Our love for others begins with our love for ourselves. We cannot truly be friends with another merely because he can "do" something for us. And we should not become the enemy of another just because he may not always help us. We have to balance our friendships, just as we balance the Yetzer Tov and the Yetzer HaRa within us. There are times when it is right to use a friend to do something for us, and times when we must be willing to give of ourselves for the sake of our friends.

Popularity and the community Friendship and mutual love form the basis for the peace and prosperity of the community. When a community is formed only for some material reason, then when the material reason passes away, the community passes away with it. But when a community is formed for the purpose of mutual help and concern, the community lasts forever.

Being popular can be a good example of a material cause. When we form a small clique in the hopes that it will make us popular, and it does not do so, the clique fades away and we turn to something else. When we become part of a friendship in a small group that is based on some material purpose, the group is good for us only so long as it serves that purpose for us. When it no longer serves us, we abandon it and turn elsewhere. We all know people who only want to be on the "winning" team. When the going gets rough, they are the first to quit.

The Jewish community is an example of a community built on true friendship and mutual love. We say of ourselves *Kol Yisrael Arevim Zeh LaZeh:* Every Jew is responsible for his fellow Jews. Whenever a Jew is in trouble or in danger, he can turn to the Jewish community and be sure of help and aid. We care for one another because of our common love for God and for God's laws.

The All-Present Perhaps it is also for this reason that the rabbis often referred to God as the "All-Present," the "One who is ever with us." When we act through true friendship, we are taking the part of God in the world, doing the work of God as we understand it. Therefore, we say that "God is with us."

A Hassidic rebbe was once asked, "Where is God in the world?" His reply was, "Wherever man lets him in." When we open ourselves to God's spirit, we let God enter the world through us. In this way we understand what the rabbis meant when they called God the All-Present.

As Jews and as members of the Jewish community, we have pledged ourselves to bring God's spirit into our lives together. And this is why letting the value of popularity control us and following the multitude to do evil are not a part of the Jewish way of life.

FRIENDSHIP AND COMMUNITY

Friendship is best based on bringing the spirit of
God into our daily lives. It requires a sense of
equality, of respect for one another. We take delight
in friendship. And we bring delight and comfort
to those around us.

True friendship is always based on feelings of equality and freedom. If Jonathan looked upon David only as a threat to his inheriting the kingship, his spirit would have been filled with jealousy and hate. It was because he looked at David and saw another human being in danger, a member of his community threatened, a fellow Jew in trouble, an equal partner in God's world being mistreated, that he was able to act in the spirit of God.

A Hassidic story told by Reb Urele of Strelisk shows how

**Between God
and man**

the spirit of God helps us to control our tendency to forget that others are our equal:

> When I was a little boy and the teacher had just begun to teach me reading, he once showed me two small letters, like square dots in the prayerbook, and said, "Urele, you see these letters side by side? That stands for the name of God. Whenever you see these two dots side by side, you must pronounce the name of God at that spot, even though it is not written out in full."
>
> I continued reading with my teacher until we came to a colon at the end of the line. The colon, too, was made up of two square dots, but instead of being side by side, they were written one above the other. I imagined that this too must be the name of God and I pronounced it at this spot. But my teacher told me:
>
> "No, no, Urele, that does not mean the name of God. Only where there are two sitting nicely side by side, where the one looks on the other as an equal—only there is the name of God; where one is under the other and the other is raised above his fellow—there the word of God cannot be." [Nine Gates, Jiri Langer]

When people join in cliques, they think of themselves as raised above others. But that is not really popularity; and the truth is that they have forgotten others. In reality they are not raising themselves above, but merely separating themselves from the community.

Our pleasure is God's pleasure It is not merely popularity in the community that is important, but increasing peace in the community. In this way, there can be a kind of popularity that is worth achieving. It is the kind that brings peace and satisfaction into the world around us. And it happens when we are popular because we are respected by our neighbors. But here the word "popular" may become confusing. Let's approach it in a different way.

The desire for popularity when taken to an extreme is evil. It leads us to follow the multitude no matter what. And it causes us to forget our own needs and the real needs of our community. Bringing pleasure to others, however, is a value worth pursuing. It is based on loving our neighbors as we love ourselves. It means giving respect and is a positive form of popularity.

This is the kind that Ḥanina had in mind when he said:

He in whom the spirit of his companions takes delight, in him the Spirit of the All-Present takes delight. [Avot 3:13]

If Ḥanina had wanted to tell us that we should try to be popular no matter what, he would have said, "He in whom his companions take delight. . . ." But instead, he said, "the *spirit* of his companions." And in this careful use of language, there is a great difference in meaning.

Ḥanina is not saying that God is pleased with those who are popular all the time. The Prophets, for example, were often far from popular. They spoke out against the people of the community, calling upon the people to change their selfish ways and turn back to the ways of God. Can we imagine that the Spirit of the All-Present was not delighted by the Prophets?

No. It is because the people heard the voice of truth in the words of the Prophets that these words were recorded and saved for all times. Even when the people did not like the Prophets, their *spirit* was touched and moved by the Prophets' message.

So, too, when we delight the spirit of our friends and neighbors, we delight the Spirit of the All-Present. When we act to bring peace, justice, and mercy into our community, we are acting in a way that brings delight and comfort to those around us. When we make friends in the true spirit of friendship, those friendships last and the spirit of our companions takes delight in us. So, too, God joins in a true friendship by delighting at its creative fruit.

Bringing peace into the world

We have spoken much about bringing peace into the world, but it often seems like an impossible task. After all, nations are still fighting wars against one another. How can one person help bring peace into the world?

The answer lies in the things that we do day by day. Each act of peace within our own lives seems a simple matter. It may only be avoiding an argument with our parents, or it may mean not arguing with a brother or a sister. But the small act brings peace into the world.

It is no wonder, then, that Rabbi Ḥanina ben Dosa felt that the Spirit of the All-Present takes delight when the spirit of our neighbors takes delight. For peace has a way of spreading in the world, the smallest act of peace can bring God's spirit closer to us and to all around us.

To achieve delight

Bringing delight to the spirit of our neighbors requires us to act in a way that will ease our neighbor's burdens and make life more pleasant. It was this that was at the base of the Prophets' pleas. Turn away from evil, the Prophets said, and you will be more pleasing to yourself, to one another, and to God. The rabbis pointed out that we should be careful to offer "the soft answer" [Ber. 17a], the answer that would cause anger to vanish.

This is good advice. Often people come to us in an angry way. When we react by being angry, too, the result can only be destructive. But turning away their anger is often not difficult. Usually giving a "soft answer" will make the angry person reasonable and willing to listen and discuss. It is a good way of increasing the peace around us.

More advice comes from Shammai, who said, "Receive all people in a cheerful manner" [Avot 1:15]. This is a reminder of the power of a smile. Smiling is very often catching, and is always helpful in turning a person's mood from one of sadness and anger to one of delight.

And finally, Ben Zoma said, "Who is honored? He who honors others" [Avot 4:1]. We should constantly try to remind ourselves that we are all equals, and that each of us deserves respect and honor. Perhaps here we can see one reason for the commandment "Honor your father and your mother." Our parents are usually the easiest people for us to honor. If we cannot honor them, we can hardly even begin to honor others. Therefore, the commandment reminds us to learn ways of honoring our parents, so that we can turn our learning to the task of honoring all around us.

Reflection

Popularity is usually a value of the marketplace. Seeking it is often based on a selfish love, and it fades with the passing of its cause. But being the delight of the spirit of others through developing true friendships is a task worthy of our entire lifetime. It is a value in which we can even say that the Spirit of the All-Present God delights. For what brings peace and well-being into the life of the community brings the Spirit of God closer to all.

A person should always give the soft answer that turns away anger, increasing peace with his community and relatives and with all people, even with the non-Jew, so that he may be loved above and well-loved on earth, and acceptable to his neighbors.
[Ber. 17a]

But you might ask, "If I am good and do not bother at all with my neighbors, will not God love me anyway?" In this regard, the rabbis taught us that there are two kinds of righteous persons:

One kind is good toward God and toward his neighbors. The other kind is good toward God and evil toward his neighbors. [Kid. 40a]

But God delights in the person who is good toward both God and his neighbors, for in that person the spirit of his companions takes delight and the Spirit of the All-Present takes delight.

In considering the kind of community that we wish to build and the way in which we hope our community to grow, it is not difficult to see that a community built on lasting friendships as opposed to "popularity" is the community that will last and endure. It is the community, like Israel, that can say, "We are responsible for one another."

17

The value of sensitivity

רַבִּי שִׁמְעוֹן בֶּן־אֶלְעָזָר אוֹמֵר. אַל תְּרַצֶּה אֶת־חֲבֵרְךָ בִּשְׁעַת כַּעֲסוֹ. וְאַל תְּנַחֲמֵהוּ בְּשָׁעָה שֶׁמֵּתוֹ מֻטָּל לְפָנָיו. וְאַל תִּשְׁאַל לוֹ בִּשְׁעַת נִדְרוֹ. וְאַל תִּשְׁתַּדֵּל לִרְאוֹתוֹ בִּשְׁעַת קַלְקָלָתוֹ:

Rabbi Simeon ben Eleazar said, Do not appease your friend in the hour of his anger, and comfort him not in the hour when his dead lies before him, and question him not in the hour of his vow, and strive not to see him in the hour of his disgrace. [Avot 4:23]

Sensitivity   You probably remember the first time you told a special secret to a friend and your friend started to tell it to everyone else you knew. You might even have called your friend "wicked" for causing you embarrassment.

Or perhaps you were so bad at playing some game that when sides were picked you were the very last one chosen, and the player choosing said glumly, "I guess you're on my side." It doesn't exactly make you feel good to be thought of as the weakest link on the team.

All of us have moments of this sort, and all of us sometimes cause embarrassment to others, too, even when we do not mean to (and sometimes we cause others embarrassment on purpose, just to be mean to them). Actually, a person has to learn how *not* to embarrass others. Learning this does not come naturally.

We are not born being sensitive to what hurts others. We have to train ourselves, even to the point of studying how others are hurt so that we may avoid hurting them. And, of course, our group has a big stake in helping us to learn to be more sensitive to others.

One of the things we said that a group must do, if it is to be successful, is to stay together. If the group begins to break up because its members do not get along with one another, then the group loses its feeling of togetherness and before long dissolves.

Keeping the group together

This is just as true of our Jewish group as of any other to which we may belong. And in the Jewish community the stakes are very high. If the community dissolves, each person is left alone; the purposes of living together fade,

ACQUIRING SENSITIVITY

We would not knowingly harm others. So, too, we would not embarrass them. But sometimes we need to exercise our imagination a bit to understand how others feel, or how we would feel in their place. To be truly sensitive we must consider not only what we do but when and how we do it.

and all the progress we have made together toward becoming a more perfect society and making a better world is lost.

So the rabbis were very concerned not only with *what* you do, but with the often harder questions of *when* you should act and *how* you should behave toward others. They taught us that sensitivity to one another will help us stay together.

A full-time task Being sensitive to one another is a full-time task. It does not even become easier when we live closely together for a long time. It is almost always difficult. Take, for example, your family.

You have lived longer with your family than with any other group to which you belong. It is for this reason that the rabbis placed such a strong emphasis on keeping the Jewish family close together, on making each family a small Jewish people. Still and all, it is difficult to remember to be kind to a brother or sister. There are times when we are naturally jealous (you might remember the story of Joseph and his fancy coat and how jealous all of his brothers were). There are times when we embarrass our parents, as well as times when our parents embarrass us (you might remember a time when a friend spent the night at your house and you both had to go to bed at *your* bedtime). Because your parents are different from all other parents, they may sometimes make you do things other parents do not think are so important.

So your family is a good example of just how difficult it is to get along with others in a sensitive way.

Sensitivity is sensible Yet it makes good sense to try to be sensitive to others. All through our study we have seen just how much we depend upon one another for all kinds of support. Our families provide us with care and food and shelter and love, even when no one else might. And the Jewish people is a kind of extended family—our Jewish community cares for those who have no families of their own, and even for those who have families. We build the community together, and sensitivity is one of the building blocks.

A FAMILY KIND OF THING

Kindness should begin at home—and spread out
from there. Respecting the feelings of brothers and
sisters cuts down needless rivalries. Appreciation
for parents binds the family closer. And the same
sensitivity binds the Jewish community together.

So it is a mitzvah to visit the sick. It is a mitzvah to comfort those who mourn. It is a mitzvah to restore calm to an angry person. It is a mitzvah to give charity. It is a mitzvah to help a person in time of need. It is a mitzvah to ransom captives. And performing these mitzvot is an act of lovingkindness—an act of the sensitive person. These acts help us to strengthen our community, to bring our people closer together.

Timing is important

Still, it is not only what you do that is important, it is when you do it. For example, if you are serving a volleyball, you begin by throwing the ball into the air. Now you wait for exactly the best moment to hit it with your hand. If you hit it too soon, it will go straight up into the air. If you wait too long, it will go straight into the net. Only when your timing is precise does the volleyball do what you want it to do.

The same is true in performing a mitzvah. If you perform it too soon, before it is needed, it will hang in the air waiting for a result that may never come. Imagine making a sick call on a friend who isn't sick—would you say, "I'm just visiting you now so that sometime in the future, when you are not feeling well, I won't have to come over and visit you"? Or imagine helping a blind woman across the street before she wanted to cross it. Would she express appreciation when she turned and said, "I really wanted to be on the other side of the street"?

Nor will performing a mitzvah too late be of much use. Waiting until a person has starved to death before giving charity to him can hardly be counted as a mitzvah. Comforting a person on the loss of a loved one who died four years ago just cannot have the same effect as comforting him when he is in need.

Mitzvot and the performance of mitzvot require proper timing. And acquiring a good sense of timing plays an important part in developing our religious awareness. Acquiring tact includes coming to know the right time for doing a mitzvah, when to speak and when to be silent.

Rabbi Simeon ben Eleazar spoke of four ways in which we might be more sensitive to others: the first involves calming an angry person; the second deals with bringing comfort to one who is in mourning; the third deals with how to treat someone taking a vow; and the fourth brings us back to the subject with which we began this chapter—the topic of embarrassment.

The hour of anger

First, Simeon said, "Do not appease your friend in the hour of his anger" [Avot 4:23].

> *When a person gives way to anger, if he is wise, his wisdom leaves him; if he is a prophet, his power of prophecy leaves him. And even if greatness was granted for him by Heaven, whoever becomes angry loses it. [Pes. 66b]*

Rage and anger eat deep into a person until everything around seems to turn sour. In a fit of anger a person may say things that he will regret long after. When someone is angry with you, it is good for you to apologize, to "give the soft answer." It is good to try to patch up differences, but timing and tact are essential.

Simeon warns us not to try to apologize or reason with a person who is in the heat of anger, for he is then controlled only by the Yetzer HaRa. "All the divisions of hell rule over the angry man" [Ned. 22a].

Instead, wait. Time your appearance with the disappearance of rage from the angry person. If you come too soon, your appearance may only make him more angry, and that is just the opposite of what you wish.

On the other hand, if you wait too long, the person who was angry may come to bear a grudge against you. He may learn to hate you in his heart. For the angry person "becomes more and more stupid" [Ned. 22b].

Seeking and receiving forgiveness

You may have some experience with people who bear grudges. Even after you apologize time and time again, they still remember everything you have done that was wrong and consider you an enemy.

The value of sensitivity 187

The rabbis have taught: It says, "You shall not hate your brother in your heart." For a person might think, "I must not strike him or beat him or curse him [but I can still hate him as an enemy]." Therefore the commandment says, "in your heart." [Arach. 16b]

When another person refuses to forgive you after you have sincerely apologized and after you have made up for any losses you might have caused, then it is the other person who is sinning.

Even though a person pays another whom he has insulted, he is not forgiven by God, until he seeks forgiveness from the one he has insulted. That person, if he does not forgive the other, is called merciless. [Mishnah, Baba K. 8:7]

We cannot control what is in another person's heart. He alone controls his heart. But we must still seek forgiveness and hope that we can turn our enemies into friends. The more often we do this when we are wrong, the more friends we will have and the better our community will be.

Sometimes, the rabbis said, even when we think that we are right in an argument, we should give in. As long as the argument is not an important one, peace is more important than winning by being right. And very often hatred grows because we are too stubborn. It is better for us to bend a little than to cause disunity and separation.

In the hour of death Rabbi Simeon also advised that we should not offer comfort to a person when "his dead lies before him." Comforting the mourner is a mitzvah. But in the very moment that a loved one dies, the mourner has a right to a time of private grief and sorrow. We should not try to comfort too hastily, for we may only cause the mourner to experience more sadness and grief.

This kind of tactfulness is referred to in the Book of Job when Job's three friends come to comfort him at the death of his loved ones.

Now when Job's three friends heard of all this evil that was come upon him, they came every one from his own place . . . to comfort

him. So they sat down with him upon the ground seven days and seven nights, and none spoke a word to him; for they saw that his grief was very great. [Job 2:11–13]

The three were so sensitive to Job's mood that they actually waited seven days and seven nights! At the end of that time, "Job spoke." And this was their sign that the time was proper for them to console Job and to comfort him.

In the face of death, there is really little that we can say. Sometimes the most tactful thing we can do is sit silently by. Just our presence can have a good effect on the person who is suffering. For death is the final separation of a person from the community, and separation is very hard to bear.

Rabbi Simeon expressed the feelings of the sensitive person. Death is like an open wound. "When his dead lies before him," a person must suffer; and we must be tactful enough to allow even for suffering.

In the time of a vow

More difficult to understand from our modern point of reference is the importance that Simeon sees in the making of a vow. "Question him not in the hour of his vow," Simeon said. We may understand this in a general way by saying that when people are in the grip of a strong feeling, so strong that they swear to do something about it, we should usually let their vow pass without remarking or discussing it.

Usually we want people to keep their promises, but there are times when we make a promise in haste and are sorry afterward that we made it. What Simeon probably meant was that we should not question a person when we hear him make a promise that he cannot keep. Our questions may be embarrassing. They may force that person to do what he really does not want to do. It is better for all if we merely keep silent. It is the tactful thing to do.

For example, suppose you hear a friend promise never to trust his parents again because they forgot to do something for him. You should not then ask questions such as, "Are you sure that you will never trust them again?" or "Who else can you trust if not your parents?" These questions may only embarrass your friend. His vow was the kind made in anger or in haste and not really meant to be honest and truthful. At least for the moment, you should let it pass, even if you disagree with it.

In the hour of embarrassment

Simeon's final piece of advice was "Strive not to see him in the hour of his disgrace."

Here Simeon is speaking of the tactless person who rushes to see what is going on that can be turned into gossip. Some people love to spread the "bad word" about others, to embarrass others. But Judaism teaches us that each human being is precious, made in the image of God, and so Simeon sees embarrassing another person as a kind of killing of a person's spirit. Whenever we are publicly embarrassed, even the blood within us reacts.

A sage taught . . . .: If anyone puts his neighbor to shame in public, it is as if he shed blood. [Rav Nahman] replied, That is well said, because we can see how the red blood [of the face] recedes and whiteness comes [as the person grows pale]. [Baba M. 58b]

If you think about how it feels to be embarrassed, whether because of something you did unintentionally or because of something that happened to you, you know how deeply embarrassment can hurt. Here, especially, there is a need for us to be sensitive to other people.

Here, too, timing and tact are important. The girls who seek out a friend just after the dance and tease her because no one would dance with her are cruel. But the girl who seeks out a friend just after the dance to comfort her because no one would dance with her is cruel, too, though not in the same way. Those who tease are cruel in an evil way. Their action is an action of the Yetzer HaRa. But the girl who tries to comfort too soon is cruel through causing embarrassment. Though she means well, her action is ill timed: it is tactless. She has failed to use her religious awareness.

ALL-IMPORTANT TIMING

A mitzvah should not be performed too early or too late. And the rabbis advise us not to try to calm a man at the height of his anger or to console him in the hour of his bereavement, or to question him when he is making a vow, or to see him when he is in disgrace. After all, how would you feel?

Before you run headlong to tell a friend how sorry you feel for him, you should first ask yourself how you might really help him—what you might really do. Otherwise, you may find that you are not really acting through your Yetzer Tov, but through your Yetzer HaRa. You might find that your bad timing is intentional and cruel. You may just want to seem "big" by comparison.

That is why Simeon warns us not to see a friend "in the hour of his disgrace." It is tactless and harmful. And it is a way of forgetting our real purpose, the goal we have of remembering how important each and every human being is, and how much peace can mean for all of us.

Reflection Just knowing that all of us are created equal and that each of us is uniquely valuable is not enough. We must learn to be sensitive to one another in our everyday dealings. To do this we have to learn how to time the performance of mitzvot so that we do things when they are supposed to be done and in the proper way.

Doing things at the proper time and with the proper attitude is what we call tact. When we are tactful, our mitzvot help others by comforting them and supporting them.

Especially in times of stress, when our emotions are frazzled—when we are angry, when we are mourning the death of a loved one, when we have made a rash promise, or when we are embarrassed by our own actions— we need more than ever the support of the people around us, the friends and family we love.We must also learn, when others undergo such stress, to be good friends and close family for them, too. Through our religious awareness we should try to find the best way of helping them, whether by word, by action, or by silence.

Whatever we do, we must not lose sight of our goal of a better community. Our actions should be directed toward bringing ourselves and our friends and our relatives back into the peaceful flow of Jewish life as soon as possible, so that the whole community can work together as one family.

18

The value of argument

כָּל מַחֲלֹקֶת שֶׁהִיא לְשֵׁם שָׁמַיִם. סוֹפָהּ לְהִתְקַיֵּם. וְשֶׁאֵינָהּ
לְשֵׁם שָׁמַיִם. אֵין סוֹפָהּ לְהִתְקַיֵּם.

*Every disagreement which is for the sake of
Heaven shall in the end lead to a permanent
result; but every disagreement which is not for
the sake of Heaven, shall not lead to a permanent result. [Avot 5:20]*

Agreement and disagreement

Living together in peace does not mean that we all must
dress the same way, feel the same way, act in the same
way, believe in the same way, eat the same way, go to the
same places at the same times—in other words, forego our
individuality.

*Only a single person was created so that we might understand the
greatness of God, for man turns out many coins with one mold, and
they are all alike to one another; but God turned out every man
with the mold of the first man, yet not one of them is like his fellow.
[Mishnah, Sanh. 4:5]*

It would be a boring world if all of us were the same. There
would be nothing new to discover in our friends and

neighbors. Everywhere we turned we would only see duplicates of ourselves—people who were us facing us. There would not be a story we did not know, or a voice we did not recognize, or a new piece of music we could not compose, or a work of art we could not create. The magic of individuality and uniqueness would have disappeared.

In the same way, it would not be healthy if we all agreed on all subjects. Each of us would lose his ability to be independent. Each of us would do whatever the group does. We would be like worker ants, all moving and acting through one common instinct. Instead, God has turned us out of the mold of humanity, giving us the gift of uniqueness.

We are unique in the way we feel and in the things in which we believe. We are unique in the way we look and the way we act. We can learn and teach. We can find interest in one another.

The price we pay for this uniqueness is disagreement. As often as not, we see the world differently from the way in which others see it. We do not always act as others would like us to act. And the way others think and act does not always agree with our own ideas and notions.

Two kinds of disagreement

Such disagreement can be either destructive or constructive. It is destructive when it leads to quarreling and fighting with little or no reason. And it is constructive when out of our disagreement, and through it, we learn something new or build something greater. Through disagreement we can lose peace and lose one another; and through disagreement we can also find one another and build a closer peace.

A good way of visualizing the two sides of disagreement is in the way we act with friends. The person who argues with his friends about what should be their favorite kind of ice cream is merely being destructive. But the person who disagrees with his friends when they are bullying someone younger is being constructive. Two friends do not have to agree on what sport is their favorite, how to brush hair, what clothes to wear, or even what religion is best. But when disagreement can lead to learning, it can be important to disagree.

Joseph Zabara, a thirteenth-century Spanish Jew, wrote: "Friendship is one heart in two bodies." If your friend is a true friend, then you do not have to worry about losing his or her friendship when you honestly disagree with an idea or action, or when you choose a separate way. And when you are a true friend, you care more about your friendship than to turn away in a moment of disagreement. A person who would say, "If you do not do what I want you to, I will not be your friend," is not much of a friend to begin with.

There is both agreement and disagreement in our community, too. People even choose different ways of believing in the same thing. There are Orthodox, Conservative, and Reform Jews. As individuals we choose which branch

In the community

DISAGREEMENTS—WHAT KIND, AND WHY?

Each of us is unique. No wonder we sometimes disagree. Disagreement is destructive when it is only pointless quarreling. But it may be constructive if it brings new evidence to light or leads us to look at things in a new way.

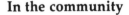

of Judaism to join according to our needs and our beliefs. Yet all are Jews, all seeking the same purposes. We are all members of a larger group, the Jewish people, which is wide enough to hold all of our separate beliefs and ways.

When we let differences such as Orthodox, Conservative, or Reform come between us, we lose sight of our highest goals and scatter into fragments like the broken pieces of a china cup. Better to let our differences serve us to help one another and bring us closer, just as the cup is in need of handle, base, and sides to be one.

Room for disagreement The rabbis taught us that some disagreements are good. When a disagreement is "for the sake of Heaven," it is good and will lead to good results. As an example, they pointed to the disagreement between Hillel and Shammai.

Shammai and Hillel each founded a school of learning. Shammai's was known as the House of Shammai, and Hillel's as the House of Hillel. In both schools the Oral Tradition was taught along with the study of Torah. But Hillel and Shammai were very different teachers.

The story is told that a nonbeliever came to Shammai with the request that Shammai teach him the whole Torah while standing on one foot [that is, in a few sentences]. Shammai drove the nonbeliever away with a yard-stick that he was holding at the time.

The nonbeliever then went to Hillel with the same request. "Teach me the Torah while you stand on one foot."

Hillel replied, "What is hateful to yourself, do not to your neighbor. That is the whole Torah and the rest is commentary. Now go and study." [Shab. 31a]

Shammai refused to water down the Torah for the non-believer, and with good reason. The Torah is very complex and requires a great deal of study to be understood in all its depth. Shammai wanted the nonbeliever to know that the study of Torah is serious. So he drove the nonbeliever away in a mocking fashion to show that he felt the nonbeliever was mocking Torah.

Hillel was softer of nature. There are many stories of his kindness and patience. He took the nonbeliever's mocking question and answered it in all seriousness.

Each in his own way was right, but the answer of Hillel was so brilliant and clear that even today we quote it as a good summary of the spirit of Torah life. Nevertheless, Shammai's reaction was also an answer, and even today when a person comes to a rabbi and asks to be converted to Judaism, the rabbi must first try to discourage the would-be convert so that he will know that the study of Judaism is a serious study. So we can see that both answers, though they disagree, were right.

Jews may be classed as Orthodox, Conservative, and Reform. But all are united in allegiance to Torah and in concern for the Jewish community. Why did Shammai answer the nonbeliever as he did? Why did Hillel answer differently? Why are both answers considered good ones?

give to charity

So it is when the sages enter the house of study, and are occupied with Torah. One says its meaning is this, and another says its meaning is that. One gives such an opinion, his fellow a different one. But they were all "given from one shepherd"—that is from Moses, who received the teaching from Him who is One and unique in the world. [Pesikta Rabbati 8a]

For the sake of Heaven Constructive disagreement is a good example of how we can turn our Yetzer HaRa to the purpose of good. All disagreements must begin with the Yetzer HaRa, for it is this impulse that divides us from others. Yet when we turn the argument to constructive use, when we learn something new or build something better as a result of our disagreement, then we say that we are acting "for the sake of Heaven."

Every disagreement which is for the sake of Heaven shall in the end lead to a permanent result. . . . Such was the disagreement between Hillel and Shammai. [Avot 5:20]

What happens in constructive disagreement is that we succeed in balancing the Yetzer HaRa, which began the disagreement, with the Yetzer Tov, which directs the disagreement back to peace. For it is the Yetzer Tov that helps us to draw near to one another.

When only the Yetzer Tov is present, no disagreement can take place. But where there is no argument, there is no growth, no change. Unless we learn to be free of others, we will always depend on them. We all know the goody-goody who never disobeys and who never argues and who never questions. The danger of such people is that they may never learn to think for themselves. Questioning and doubt are the beginnings of wisdom; and disagreements are necessary for growth.

Yet disagreements that begin and end with the Yetzer HaRa are destructive instead of helpful. In the end they lead to no permanent result. We have all experienced such arguments from time to time. Perhaps you once quarreled with your parents and got so angry that you eventually forgot what the argument was all about in the first place. You might have gone on sputtering and arguing, even though you knew that there was no permanent end to be gained, that you were just saying words for the sake of saying them. Letting the Yetzer HaRa get out of control results in such an argument, which is not "for the sake of Heaven."

The best path is the one between the two extremes. Disagreement that is begun by the Yetzer HaRa can be turned to useful purpose through a blending in of the Yetzer Tov. When both are used and controlled, the results may very well be permanent and good. Constructive disagreements can produce friendships and strength within the community. These disagreements can result in the formulation of new ideas and theories that provide us new insights into the world around us.

Pirke Avot also speaks of the destructive disagreement:

Every disagreement which is not for the sake of Heaven . . . shall not lead to a permanent result. . . . Such was the disagreement of Koraḥ and all his company. [Avot 5:20]

How do we know that the disagreement of Korah and all his company was not for the sake of Heaven? One clue is found in the way in which we are told about Korah. In speaking of the long dispute between Hillel and Shammai, Avot mentions both their names. But in speaking of the rebellion of Korah, only the side of Korah and his followers is mentioned.

The rabbis were teaching us in this way that a disagreement can only be for the sake of Heaven when there are two sides that disagree openly, each side listening to the arguments of the other side and replying in turn. This was the case in the arguments between Hillel and Shammai.

But Korah listened to Moses with a closed ear. He did not pay attention to any of Moses' words. For Korah, the disagreement was a way of becoming a leader. He was not interested in the truth or falsity of his arguments, only in seeing his side win. When we stop listening to the other side of an argument, we stop disagreeing honestly, and begin disagreeing selfishly.

This is as true for the community as it is for the individual. Note that Pirke Avot speaks of "Korah *and all his company*." And with regard to groups the rabbis said:

כָּל כְּנֵסְיָה שֶׁהִיא לְשֵׁם שָׁמַיִם. סוֹפָהּ לְהִתְקַיֵּם. וְשֶׁאֵינָה לְשֵׁם שָׁמַיִם. אֵין סוֹפָהּ לְהִתְקַיֵּם:

Any assembly which is for the sake of Heaven shall in the end lead to permanent results, but any assembly which is not for the sake of Heaven shall not lead to a permanent result. [Avot 4:14]

The community and results Whenever a group of people such as the "company of Korah" come together solely out of jealousy, fear, hatred, selfishness, or one of the other disguises of the Yetzer HaRa, their community lasts for a very short time and nothing truly comes of it. The rabbis tell us that every man in Korah's company was there for only one reason: to become the high priest. Now, since there can be only one high priest, we can imagine what kind of a community it would have been if Korah's company had come to power.

But when an assembly comes together for the sake of Heaven, to work together, it leads to permanent results. Good examples of this are charitable organizations, universities and colleges, service organizations, community agencies, religious schools, synagogues and temples, and youth groups. As long as such assemblies do not forget to keep an open ear to disagreement and argument and to keep an eye on their real goals and aims, they serve us well and provide us with permanent results.

What is most important in the assembly for the sake of Heaven is providing a place for open thinking and planning. When honest people stand facing one another and discussing the real problems that concern all of us—the problems of our society and of our times—we can hope for permanent results. We can hope to learn and grow together, each of us sharing his or her own special ideas with all others.

"Every disagreement which is for the sake of heaven shall **Reflection** . . . lead to a permanent result." The truth of the matter is that good arguments are the arguments that come closest to the roots of our very way of life. When we discuss and

debate the meaning of good and evil, we are taking up a disagreement that has been honestly faced for centuries and that will continue to be faced in the future.

When we consider the differences between a true and a false friend and argue which friend is true and which false, we are taking up a disagreement that is a part of the inner structure of our life as a people.

When we consider and debate whether or not to hurt our enemies, whether or not to help those in trouble, whether or not to speak out against injustice, and whether or not to give charity, we are taking up disagreements that are based on the values of our Jewish community.

These questions are often unanswerable. We may argue, but we cannot solve them totally. Neither can we solve them simply by agreeing to agree. In the case of unanswerable questions—such as "Why do people who are evil succeed so often?"—our disagreement leads to a different kind of result.

By disagreeing, we keep the question alive. We raise it above the commonplace and make it an important issue. We cause others to consider it and seek answers to it. The result of our disagreement is an effort to find the truth.

By creating this atmosphere of searching, by constantly seeking to determine what is for the sake of Heaven and what is not, we keep our minds ever on the future. We keep our eyes wide open to what is possible for us, to what we may do to make our world one in which all people are concerned with one another.

The disagreement that is for the sake of Heaven, then, serves to bring us closer together. It helps us to become one again, just as we were in the moment when God created us in His image.

It was the knowledge that disagreement can lead to greater agreement and to the discovery of truth that led the rabbis to say: "These and those"—meaning, both sides of an argument for the sake of heaven—"are each the words of the Living God" [Erub. 13b].

19

The value of Torah

רַבִּי אֶלְעָזָר בֶּן־עֲזַרְיָה אוֹמֵר. אִם אֵין תּוֹרָה אֵין דֶּרֶךְ אֶרֶץ.
אִם אֵין דֶּרֶךְ אֶרֶץ אֵין תּוֹרָה. אִם אֵין חָכְמָה אֵין יִרְאָה.
אִם אֵין יִרְאָה אֵין חָכְמָה. אִם אֵין דַּעַת אֵין בִּינָה. אִם אֵין
בִּינָה אֵין דַּעַת. אִם אֵין קֶמַח אֵין תּוֹרָה. אִם אֵין תּוֹרָה אֵין
קֶמַח:

> *Rabbi Eleazar ben Azariah said, Where there*
> *is no Torah, there are no manners; and where*
> *there are no manners, there is no Torah. . . .*
> *Where there is no flour, there is no Torah,*
> *where there is no Torah there is no flour.*
> *[Avot 3:21]*

Religion and mankind

The saying of Rabbi Eleazar is like the performance of a juggler. With only a slight motion of the juggler's hands the balls seem to be suspended in midair and moving all at once. In the same way, Eleazar juggles the ideas of Torah and manners, Torah and flour.

From the word "flour," we know that he is speaking symbolically. Flour stands for our daily bread, the feeding of our bodies. Torah, by comparison, must stand for the feeding of our souls—our religion.

The same is true of the comparison between Torah and manners. Manners here stand for the everyday way of life we choose. Torah represents our highest standards, our goals, our ethics, and our laws—again, our religion.

Of course, manners may be either good or bad. When we use just the word "manners," we are usually speaking of *good* manners—a sensitive and compassionate way of behaving in the presence of others.

A world without Torah We often hear people say that having good manners is all that a person needs to make the world a peaceful place. They may say, "Being Jewish just separates me from the rest of the world." Or they may say, "I just want to be human."

What these people forget is that the natural state of just being "human" is an animal state. It is a state in which kindness hardly ever survives. At our most human we are most like wild animals that fight and claw at one another when hungry and that repay kindness with evil. Good manners are fine, but without the protection of Torah, without laws to guide us, they do not remove us far enough from our animal state. To show this the rabbis told a story of an old man and a serpent:

One cold day an old man left his fireside to walk through his fields. In his hand was a stick he used to help him over the rough ground and also for protection against the beasts of the field. As he walked, he noticed a snake lying very still on the ground beside his path. He raised up the stick to kill it, but the snake did not move. It was then that the man realized that the snake was frozen from the cold.

The old man felt pity for the snake. He raised its frozen body from the ground and held it close to his own body to warm it. Soon the snake grew stronger, but still it pretended to be weak. Then all at once, the snake wound itself around the old man and began to crush him.

The old man cried out in fear, "Do you wish to kill me? I have just saved your life. Have you no gratitude?"

The snake laughed. "The Torah says that the snake shall bruise the heel of man," said the snake. "I must kill you as is the way of snakes with men."

The old man was sore afraid. He pleaded with the snake. But the snake laughed. Then he asked the snake to go with him to a court of law to have the case judged.

"Who will be the judge?" asked the snake.

"Let us walk along the road," said the old man, "and the first we meet shall judge."

The snake, very sure of winning his case, agreed to go along. So the old man started off down the road with the snake still wound tightly about him.

On the road, the old man and the snake met a strong ox resting after working hard all day. The old man approached the ox.

"Tell the snake that it is wrong to kill me," said the old man. "I have just saved his life and common manners say that the snake should now save mine."

"It says in the Torah that snake and man are enemies," the snake replied. "Therefore, I must be right to crush him to death."

The ox agreed with the snake. "You did a kind deed," said the ox to the man, "but the snake must return it with an evil deed. In this world we always return good with evil."

The snake tightened his hold on the old man. But just as the old man began to cry aloud in pain, a donkey happened by. "Let us put the case to the donkey," the old man said between his teeth clenched in pain. The snake smiled and flashed his forked tongue.

And when the story was told again, the donkey agreed with the snake. "To return good with evil is the natural way," the donkey added. "It is the way of animals. He is best who is strongest. Of what use are manners in the real world of claw and fang?"

"This is no fair judgment," said the old man. "Let us put the case but one more time to judgment."

In the sky the sun had almost fallen. The shadows of the city of Jerusalem were long and dark across the tops of the hill.

"See, it is late," said the snake, "and I am hungry for I have not eaten since you saved my life. This final judgment and then you die."

As they moved down the road seeking a last judge, a strange sight presented itself at the side of the road. A noble young man stood near a large hole in the ground. The young man had lost his beautiful walking stick in the pit. He instructed his servants to fill the pit with water, and when they had done so, the stick floated to the top, and the young man reached it easily.

"Here is a wise one," the old man said. "Let him be our last judge."

"So be it," said the snake.

The young man listened as the two spoke. The old man recounted how he had saved the life of the snake. The snake also explained that it was his duty to kill the old man. The young man was silent a moment, then he spoke.

"First," he told the snake, "you must climb down from the old man, for it says in the Torah that when two are judged, neither shall have the advantage."

"Now," he asked the snake, "why do you want to kill the old man who saved your life?"

"It says in the Torah," said the snake, "You shall bruise the heel of man."

"It also says in the Torah," said the young judge, turning to the old man, "that man shall bruise the head of the serpent."

The old man raised up the stick, which he had carried all this time. He hit the serpent over the head and killed it.

"Now I understand," the old man said to his young judge, "there are no manners in the world, except those which are protected by the law of Torah."

The noble young man, none other than the teenage Solomon, son of King David of Jerusalem, smiled. [Tanḥ. B.]

Having good manners is a refinement of being human. But having manners requires us to have goals or values that support them. Consider a ticket line at a movie theatre. The manners that we observe in buying tickets dictate that the first person to come should be the first served and that everyone thereafter should be served in turn. We are all impatient, we all want to be next; still, we display good manners and wait our turn. We are annoyed, then, when someone "cuts in" on the line, or when someone pushes ahead of us. We say that he is not being fair—but we would have to agree that he is being human!

The law protects us—not the law of the land, surely, for in few if any localities is there a law specifically forbidding a person to cut into a ticket line; but the law of our religion. In the Torah, we have the commandment to love others as we love ourselves and the teaching that all are created equal. The Torah is our guide to good manners and our protection from bad manners.

So Rabbi Eleazar's statement reads, "Where there is no Torah, there are no manners." And we may read it to mean that where there is no religion or tradition to teach us a set of standards and values to control our actions, our actions will not be considerate of the needs of others.

One of the sages of the Talmud taught us that a person who has studied much Torah, who understands and loves the commandments, but does not live by them is like a horse with no reins. The Torah may ride on such a horse for a short time, but soon the horse throws the rider over its head.

"Where there are no manners . . ."

On the other hand, a person who has studied much Torah and who puts the Torah into practice is like a horse with reins. The rider, Torah, directs this horse to and fro, and the horse receives direction with pleasure [ARN 24].

The second part of Rabbi Eleazar's statement—"Where there are no manners, there is no Torah"—tells us that practical life must come first. Unless a person is willing to live by rules, the Torah will be of little use. Only if a person decides that there is a need for manners in the world will that person find the ways of Torah.

So the first step is "doing what is right in God's sight" [Exod. 15:26].

> That is, what is right in business, or in buying and selling. And so you may learn that the one who conducts business, and buys and sells, in truth and honesty, and who is pleasing to others, is regarded as if that person had fulfilled the whole Torah. [Mechilta, Vayetze, Beshallah]

When a person obeys the Law simply by following the

manners of others who are good, then his actions are every bit as good as those of someone who acts because of the Law. In this way the group can help even the most ignorant person to live a good life. Those of us who study provide an example for those who do not.

When we see that a person who has studied Torah acts with no sensitivity, or fails to act according to the principles of the Torah, then we are tempted to say, "What difference does it make how I act?" But if we see that a person who has studied the Torah acts in a kind way, bringing happiness to those around him, then we are more likely to say, "I will act in that way, also." This, the rabbis taught us, is the way of human nature.

> It is said that when [Moses' brother] Aaron was on the road, and met a man who was known to be evil, he would greet the man, saying, Shalom to you.
> The next day, if that man wanted to do evil, he said, "If I were to do this thing, how could I then lift up my eyes and look at Aaron? I would be ashamed before him, for he gave me a greeting of peace." So the man would hold back from doing evil. [ARN 12]

But how do manners lead to Torah? The best example of this is shown in a story that we studied in Chapter 1—the story of Simeon and the pearl. In the end, when Simeon returned the pearl to its rightful owner, the owner was overwhelmed by Simeon's manners. And the surprised owner's response was: "Blessed be the God of Simeon ben of Shetah."

As with Simeon and with Aaron, our manners, when they are Torah-based, lead others to the Torah. So the rabbis taught:

THE WAY OF PEACE AND BLESSING

How does the knowledge of Torah show? In truthfulness and fair dealing. In doing our part. In keeping the peace and helping make peace among others.

Let a person first do good deeds, and then ask God for the knowledge of the Torah. [Tan. d. b. El., p. 31]

The last part of the saying of Rabbi Eleazar has become famous as a proverb. It begins "Where there is no flour, there is no Torah . . .,"

There are parallel sayings in other traditions, too. For example, the Hindu master Vivekananda (1863–1902) said, "First bread, and then religion. No dogmas will satisfy the cravings of hunger."

Of course, Rabbi Eleazar probably had something more in mind. While it is true that one must eat in order to study, Eleazar was speaking, as we have said, in a symbolic way.

In the midst of poverty, a person is forced to think only of the needs of the moment. When faced with the possibility of starving to death, there is no time for manners, values, or Torah. A person reduces himself to concentrating on the bare necessities—food, clothing, and shelter. We cannot help a poor person by offering to teach him Hebrew, even if he is Jewish. We must first offer assistance of a more basic kind.

But there is more than one kind of poverty. Just when we come to understand what Rabbi Eleazar had in mind when he said, "Where there is no flour, there is no Torah," the tables are turned and he continues: ". . . where there is no Torah, there is no flour." And here is a new kind of poverty, the deprivation not of food, but of Torah.

Without the Torah, our lives would be poor. We would suffer from a hunger of the spirit. The Torah has provided such richness to the world that we speak of it as the "crown of Torah," and compare it to the crowns of priesthood and of kingship.

"Where there is no flour . . ."

"Where there is no Torah . . ."

רַבִּי שִׁמְעוֹן אוֹמֵר. שְׁלֹשָׁה כְתָרִים הֵן. כֶּתֶר תּוֹרָה וְכֶתֶר כְּהֻנָּה וְכֶתֶר מַלְכוּת. וְכֶתֶר שֵׁם טוֹב עוֹלֶה עַל גַּבֵּיהֶן:

Rabbi Simeon said, There are three crowns: the crown of Torah, the crown of priesthood, and the crown of kingship; but the crown of a good name is above them all. [Avot 4:17]

The value of Torah 209

How can Simeon say that there are three crowns and then name four? The answer is that the crown of a good name flows from the crown of Torah.

Why does it not come from the crown of priesthood? Because the priesthood refers directly to the line of Aaron and his followers, and so it is not open to just anyone.

The same is true of the crown of kingship, which is granted only to kings. Like the crown of priesthood, this crown of royalty is merely a question of earthly power, which comes and goes.

But the power of Torah is everlasting. It is open to all. Each and every Israelite can wear the crown of Torah. All are invited to study it. All are asked to hear it read week by week. A person gains wisdom by means of Torah. And through the study of Torah a person learns how to create a good name for himself.

Reflection   Through manners, we create for ourselves the "crown of a good name." And our manners are not just a matter of being human. They are derived from the learning and teaching of our people. Our manners are Jewish manners. And through our actions, we express them to the world at large.

But before we can express those manners, we must know them. We cannot wait to study, our study must begin now—now, when the soul and the mind are hungry. If we wait until they are starved, we will have waited too long. So we must avoid the poverty of the spirit that is the greatest of all the world's hungers.

Of course, you yourself must decide to do something about it. Only you can choose to make the Torah the flour that feeds your mind and nourishes your soul. And the way to do this is by *studying* Torah, the "tree of life to those who hold it fast" [Prov. 3:18].

20

The value of peace

הִלֵּל אוֹמֵר. הֱוֵי מִתַּלְמִידָיו שֶׁל אַהֲרֹן. אוֹהֵב שָׁלוֹם וְרוֹדֵף שָׁלוֹם. אוֹהֵב אֶת־הַבְּרִיּוֹת וּמְקָרְבָן לַתּוֹרָה:

Hillel said, Be of the disciples of Aaron, loving peace and pursuing peace, loving your fellow creatures, and drawing them near to the Torah. [Avot 1:12]

Loving and pursuing peace

These words of Hillel may seem a plea to the nations of the world to end wars. But Hillel's advice is not a plea to nations, but a plea to each of us personally. We know this because Hillel follows the first part of his statement with the words "loving your fellow creatures, and drawing them near to the Torah." In addition, Hillel's words were originally directed to his students, a group of individuals who had no real power in shaping the policies of the nations of the world.

Indeed, Hillel's advice to love and pursue peace is addressed to *you* as an individual. And since you might question how this might be done, Hillel continued: "by loving your fellow creatures, and drawing them near to the Torah."

Hillel felt that the best example of a person who loves and pursues peace by loving his neighbors and drawing them to Torah was Aaron, the brother of Moses.

When two people had quarreled with each other, Aaron would go and sit down with one of them and say to him "My son, the fellow you have quarreled with feels awful that he has quarreled. It is my fault, he said to me."

He would sit with him until he had removed all hatred from his heart, and then Aaron would sit with the other one and say to him: "My son, the fellow you have quarreled with feels awful that he has quarreled. It is my fault, he said to me."

He would sit with him until he had removed all hatred from his heart. And when the two men met each other, they would embrace, and kiss each other. [ARN 12]

Ways of seeking peace

Aaron did not hesitate when it came to bringing peace between man and man in Israel. He went to seek ways of bringing peace. He actively pursued peace. The fact of the matter is that we cannot hesitate in the case of peace—we must *pursue* it. The need for peace is so great that waiting will not do.

So Rabbi Simeon ben Eleazar said:

If a person sits in his own place and is inactive, how can he pursue peace in Israel between man and man? Let him instead go forth from his place and move around in the world and pursue peace in Israel, as it is said, seek peace and pursue it. Now what does that mean? Seek it in your own house, and pursue it in other places. [ARN 12]

Peace in your own house

The place to begin is at home, with your family. You may think immediately of the commandment to "Honor your father and mother," and realize how important that commandment is regarding bringing peace into the family.

Even if you disagree with the advice your mother and father give you and feel that their requests are unfair, you should nevertheless obey them out of honor—or, at the very least, protest in a kind way.

Peace should also be the goal when dealing with broth-

PEACE AT HOME

Today, as in Aaron's time, we can "seek peace and pursue it." By getting along peacefully with brothers and sisters we honor our parents. We also help make our homes pleasant places, centers of peace in our communities.

ers and sisters. Brothers and sisters often fall into arguing with one another. To our parents these arguments are very disturbing, even when they do not disturb us greatly. Most parents try very hard not to favor one of their children over another. Parents try very hard to get along with their children, too. It troubles them, then, when their children seem not to try to get along with each other. One way of honoring our parents is not fighting among ourselves.

Peace in the home is such an important Jewish value that it even has a special name, *Shalom Bayit*. Rabbi Nathan in his commentary on Pirke Avot taught that "if one brings peace into the home, the Bible accounts it as though peace were brought to all Israel" [ARN 28]. And if you have established peace at home, that is still not enough; you have to help others to live together peacefully, too.

שָׁלוֹם בַּיִת

Again, Aaron is the best example of one who pursues peace to the extent of bringing Shalom Bayit to others.

Aaron the peacemaker

If Aaron learned that a husband and wife were about to divorce, he would hurry to the husband and say, "I come because I hear that you and your wife are not getting along, and that you wish to divorce. But think of this: if you should divorce your present wife and marry another, you cannot be sure that your marriage will be better. For at the first quarrel that you have with your second wife, she will remind you that you are quarrelsome and no good, otherwise your first marriage would not have ended in divorce. Let me be a pledge that you and your present wife can be happy if you will both try."
[Legends 3:329]

Thousands of marriages were saved by Aaron's pleading and prodding. And usually when Aaron brought together those who had quarreled and were on the brink of divorce, the couple would name their first son Aaron in honor of the high priest who had saved their marriage.

Legend tells us that when Aaron died, there were no less than 80,000 Jewish children who were named Aaron in this way [ARN 12].

Bringing peace to the community In the example of Aaron we can see that the pursuit of peace within the community is to be praised. If one is in power and can avoid war, that is even more to be praised.

When God commanded Moses to make war on Sihon, Moses sent messengers of peace first. Then God said, "I ordered you to make war and instead you make overtures of peace." But God did not punish Moses. The Talmud remarks, "How great then are words of peace. If Israel disobeyed God for the sake of peace and yet God was not angry with them" [Tanḥ. B.].

The peace of our community depends on the love of each person for each other. If, instead of fighting when we feel the inner urge to quarrel, we send messengers of peace in the form of kind words, then we serve the cause of peace. But it is only the love for our fellow creatures that can urge us to send the message of peace instead of the words of trouble.

Learning to direct our actions to peace by loving our fellow creatures is at the heart of a famous story told of the Spanish Jewish poet Ibn Nagrela (993-1055):

Ibn Nagrela was a close friend of the king of Moslem Spain. Though the king was Moslem and Ibn Nagrela Jewish, yet their differences did not keep them from loving one another. But their love for one another did make for a great deal of jealousy among the Moslem poets in the king's court.

One time one of these jealous men came before the king to demand justice.

"What wrong has been done to you?" the king asked.

"The Jew, Ibn Nagrela, has stolen a poem which I wrote to call it his own," the poet reported. "He has even dared to read it before your

majesty. I beg you now, O King, to have his tongue cut out for this crime."

"We shall see," the king replied. Ibn Nagrela was summoned to the king's presence immediately.

"What have you to say to this charge?" the king asked his Jewish friend.

"I am innocent, Your Majesty," Ibn Nagrela said.

"And how can you prove your innocence?" the king asked.

"In this way," Ibn Nagrela replied. Then he drew forth the original manuscript of his poem. "Here is my first draft, and upon it are all the markings and changes which I made to better the poem in creating it. All of my work is here to be seen, from the first rough form until the final work which I read before the king."

"And you," the king said to the poet who had accused Ibn Nagrela, "can you show me your original work?"

But the jealous poet withered. "There is none," he admitted, quietly.

"Then your punishment is in the hands of Ibn Nagrela," the king said. And turning to his friend, he continued, "Cut out the evil tongue of this man, as he would have cut out yours."

Later that day the king passed the room of Ibn Nagrela and heard the sound of laughter coming from it. Opening the door, he was greatly surprised to find the two poets, Moslem and Jew, laughing and playing a game of chess together.

"Ibn Nagrela," the king said, "this man is your enemy. Why have you not removed his evil tongue?"

"But I have, Your Majesty," Ibn Nagrela replied. "I have removed his evil tongue and replaced it with a kind one."

There is much to be learned from this story in terms of bringing peace to our community. Let us consider Ibn Nagrela's alternatives. If he had cut out the tongue of his accuser, then the jealousy that the other poets felt toward Ibn Nagrela, because of his friendship with the king, would have turned to downright hatred.

Then, too, Ibn Nagrela could have left his accuser alone but remained his enemy. He could have caused his false accuser great shame among the people of the court by bragging and boasting about the king's judgment. But a person who brags about someone else's defeat is not one who loves his fellow creatures.

Kind words are "messengers of peace." So, too, are kind actions. Peacemaking may require us to lay aside hatred and bitterness, even if they seem called for. How do you think Aaron persuaded others to follow the "way of the good heart" (see Chapter 11)? How did Ibn Nagrela follow it? Did he also follow Rabbi Simeon's advice?

To the king's way of thinking, revenge was the proper solution. Yet to Ibn Nagrela's religious way of thinking, it was no solution at all. The only solution for a person who loved his fellow creatures was to turn the enemy into a friend. This is what Ibn Nagrela did. He sent forth the "message of peace" even when the "message of war" had been commanded by the king.

We can only imagine the outcome of all this, although we do not have to imagine too hard. Probably the Moslem poet became Ibn Nagrela's friend for life. And probably he was a loyal friend, too. He might have helped to ease the tension between the other Moslem poets at the king's court and Ibn Nagrela. So we can see how the action of turning an enemy into a friend can help us to increase peace within our community.

Drawing others to Torah But what does Hillel mean when he asks us to draw others near to the Torah? Actually, Hillel was speaking of Torah in the broad sense. Not just the Ḥumash, the Five Books of Moses, but the tradition and values of our people, the "tree of life" to which we must hold fast. The best means we have for drawing others near to Torah is for us to act according to the Jewish values that we have been discussing. Then all who come into contact with us will be coming close to Torah. Every place we go, the Torah will be with us. And in everything we do, the Torah will be present. In this way, we teach others by our example. Naturally, in order for us to set an example, we must first study our tradition to see what kind of an example we should set. In this light, the Talmud says, "Students of the wise enlarge peace in the world" [Ber. 64a]. Our study of Judaism is a valuable way of pursuing peace because through it we learn the everyday path to peace, the path of the good heart.

Everyday in the prayer service, we recite our prayer for the coming of an age of peace: "May He who creates peace in the heavens bring peace to us and all Israel." Our prayer not only stands as the expression of our need for peace, but it foresees a future time when peace will prevail throughout the world.

One of our noblest beliefs as Jews is the belief in the coming of the Messiah. In explaining how we might recognize the Messiah, the rabbis said of him: "The opening of his lips is for blessing and peace." Many have claimed to be the true Messiah, but none has yet provided this mark: the coming of the age of peace.

Yet this is our dream for the future. It is the ultimate message of our Prophets and the ultimate goal of our way of life.

DREAM FOR THE FUTURE

A world at peace is the ultimate hope of Judaism, its dream for mankind. The prayer for peace is central in our prayer service. The path of peace is the daily path of the good heart.

For behold, I create new heavens
And a new earth;
And the former things shall not be remembered,
Nor come into mind.

It shall come to pass that, before they call, I will answer,
And while they are yet speaking, I will hear.
The wolf and the lamb shall feed together,
And the lion shall eat straw like the ox;
And dust shall be the serpent's food.
They shall not hurt nor destroy
In all My holy mountain,
Saith the Lord. [Isa. 65:17, 24–25]

Reflection A passage in the Psalms reads, "There is a future for the man of peace" [Psalms 37:37]. The person who loves peace and pursues it is the person who looks into the future and sees the possibility of peace for all. But more than that, the pursuer of peace is the person who seeks peace each and every day, at home and in the world at large.

To be a pursuer of peace, you must come to "love your neighbor as yourself," even to the point of turning enemies into friends. And in your actions toward others, you must try to draw them nearer to the Torah by remaining yourself close to the teachings and the laws of your people.

To this, we can add the teachings of a modern sage, Rav Kook (1865-1935). When asked how he was able to love all people equally, he replied in the following manner: There is a sin that is known as *Sinat Hinnam*, hating a person who does not deserve to be hated. But in our time, there is need of a new mitzvah to be called *Ahavat Hinnam*, loving a person who does not deserve to be loved. In our day to be a true Rodef Shalom, a person who truly pursues peace, we must practice love for all—those who agree with us, and those who disagree with us; those we like and those we dislike—we must practice Ahavat Hinnam.

אַהֲבַת
חִנָּם

21

The value of labor

רַבִּי טַרְפוֹן אוֹמֵר.
לֹא עָלֶיךָ הַמְּלָאכָה לִגְמֹר. וְלֹא אַתָּה בֶּן־חוֹרִין לְהִבָּטֵל
מִמֶּנָּה.

*Rabbi Tarphon used to say, It is not up to you
to complete the work, yet you are not free to
abstain from it. [Avot 2:21]*

Doing the task

The beaver industriously gathers aspen and birch, cutting young trees with its incisor teeth, turning the trees into small logs and the logs into a tightly plastered shelter. Working with its fellow beavers, it builds a dam to protect the community from the onslaught of spring river flooding. It finds a mate and has children. It has the instinct and sense to warn other beavers as danger approaches by slapping its broad tail against the water's surface. The beaver is totally engaged in the everyday work of living, whether it be gathering food or storing wood beneath the ice for future use.

In a sense, the beaver looks beyond its daily task. Of course, it does have a concept of a future—for example, the beaver knows to store food for the winter when food is scarce. But its concept of the future is a limited one.

As human beings we have the ability to see beyond our daily tasks and ask the question, "Where am I going? What is ahead of me if I keep to this path?"

The danger Having this ability to question is both fortunate and unfortunate. It is fortunate because it means that we can choose for ourselves tasks worthy of our best abilities. We can see what we would like to do with our lives and work and plan and finally do these things. For example, you may wish to become a lawyer. You can easily figure the number of years ahead of you during which you will prepare yourself to be a lawyer. You know that to reach your goal, you will have to keep your mind on it during all those years and through all that study and practice. In this way, it is fortunate that you can visualize a future and work toward it.

How is it unfortunate? It is unfortunate when the task we set is so great that it discourages us. For example, most of us want to be good Jews. We want to use our lives in doing the work of justice, in performing acts of mercy and Gemilut Hasadim, in bringing peace into the world around us, in promoting Shalom Bayit, or peace in our homes, and in building a strong community for our own sakes and for the sake of our children. But when we consider the size of the task and the long years all of this requires, we begin to wonder: what can *one person* do?

BIG QUESTIONS

Like the animals, we must work to live. But we can look ahead and choose our lifework. Do you know what line of endeavor you might like to pursue? Other good choices may occur to you as you grow old.

Yet we must do something toward completing the task, even when we know that we cannot finish it. Each of us has a unique contribution to make, and each of us is a force within our community. In choosing *not* to make a contribution—that is, in becoming too easily discouraged and avoiding responsibility—we are not just being neutral, we are actually being negative. We are denying the world and the community that which is inside of us, the part that only we may play.

Instead, we should do whatever we can. In the words of Rabbi Tarphon:

> *It is not up to you to complete the work, yet you are not free to abstain from it.* [Avot 2:21]

The Megillah, the Book of Esther, tells us that Mordecai came to Queen Esther to warn her of Haman's plot to destroy the Jewish people. Mordecai told Esther that saving the community was up to her, that she had to change the king's mind in some way.

Yet Esther was afraid. No one was allowed to enter the king's presence unless first summoned by the king himself. The penalty for barging in was death. "What good," Esther might have argued, "will my death be to the community?"

It may also be that Esther was afraid of what the king might do if he found out that she was Jewish. She was safe in the castle, as queen; she did not want to risk her own future in order to be a heroine. "After all," she may well have told herself, "this task is too large for one person alone. Why should I risk everything to gain little or nothing?"

But Mordecai argued:

> *Do not think that you will escape here in the king's house any more than the rest of the Jews. For if you altogether hold your peace at this time, then relief and deliverance will arise to the Jews from another source.* [Esther 4:13–14]

"And who knows," Mordecai said finally, "whether you

have not come to this place and time for just this purpose?'' [Esther 4:14].

We do not know No matter how hard we think about it, we cannot really say why we were created. We do not know why we were born into one family and not into another. We do not know what purpose we were meant to serve on this earth. We do not know why we were born into this age instead of another, why we were born free and not slaves, why in this country and not in another, why male or female, why lucky or unlucky. These things are beyond our knowledge; only God knows why.

But we do know that each of us has a part to play that is unique and special. When we look at a painting by Rembrandt, we recognize it as a special contribution that only Rembrandt could have made. When we read the works of Spinoza, or of Freud, we see in them the hand of Spinoza and of Freud.

No better example of unique service could be found than that of Leo Baeck (1873-1956), a rabbi who survived a Nazi concentration camp through an error in bookkeeping. (Another Baeck was mistakenly put to death in his place.)

Before Rabbi Baeck was placed in the concentration camp, and while he knew what lay ahead for him—incarceration and probable death—he had many chances to escape to safety. Yet he refused to desert the community. Day after day he performed small bits of the task of helping fellow Jews to escape and the rest to remain united.

One time he led a group of children to England and safety. Once in England, he was urged not to return, not to place himself again in the hands of the Nazis controlling

Germany. But Rabbi Baeck refused. Instead, he returned to Germany to continue his work.

Sometimes we use discouragement as a ruse, a clever way of tricking ourselves. We see that the task is difficult, and so we say, "How can one person hope to accomplish it? It is too much for me." And we do nothing.

We know that we could at least begin the work if we wanted to, but instead we trick ourselves into believing that the work is beyond us.

Of course, if Rembrandt had done the same thing—if he had seen that the task of reproducing life through his paintings was too difficult for any person to do—we would never have the treasure of his work. This is the easy way out of working, and we human beings have the tendency to be lazy.

It is for this reason that Rabbi Tarphon said that "you are not free to abstain" from your work. The key to his statement is the word "free." For our freedom depends on our working. A person who stops working through laziness loses his freedom. One commentator, Isaac Abravanel (1437–1508), remarked:

You are not truly free when you abstain. . . . If you neglect the work, then in one way or another, you will not be a "free person." Slowly, subtly, you will come to conform, to be ruled by the values of the marketplace alone.

Each of us has a niche to fill, our own special work to do. If we do not do it, the time for it may pass us by. We cannot allow discouragement to trick us into neglecting our task. If we do, we lose our freedom of choice and action, we lose a precious part of ourselves.

Here is where we reach one of Judaism's deepest and most essential teachings: you become yourself only through independent thinking and searching and through the acts that you perform. When you give up your individuality, you cease to be a free person and become one of the herd.

We must all look inside ourselves for guidance. We should not say, "I will leave the deep thinking to someone else." That is the ruse, the trick that we play upon ourselves. What we really are saying is, "I will give up my freedom and let others control my life; I am willing to be enslaved."

We can only become truly free when we realize that, when it comes to the work we must do, we are "not free to abstain from it."

Of course, not all tasks are equal. Some are more difficult and others simpler. Some people's work seems more worthwhile than that of others in our sight. We see the great writer Leo Tolstoi, for example, in a different light than, say, Arthur Conan Doyle, the creator of the Sherlock Holmes detective stories. Yet in the end, all work is worthy of reward.

Not all tasks are equal

The rabbis taught us that the reward of all Israel is the World to Come. Just as when we set our sights on becoming a lawyer or doctor, a scientist or engineer, our reward is in our individual accomplishment, so the reward of living a good life is in the good life that we have lived and how it has brought all the world closer to the ideal world that is the dream of the Jewish people.

How can we know that this is so? In answer to this question the rabbis pointed to an interesting fact: the Torah mentions a reward for only two commandments, the greatest and the least. The greatest commandment is "Honor your father and mother," and for fulfilling this commandment the Torah promises us long life. The least commandment is to "spare the mother bird, while taking eggs from her nest," and for fulfilling this commandment the Torah also promises long life.

Now, if long life is promised for both the greatest commandment and the least, then the commandments should all be seen as equal!

A Ḥassidic rabbi was once asked, "Which is the most important mitzvah to fulfill?" He answered, "The mitzvah that you are doing at the moment that you are doing it!"

Each task that is before us must be performed with all of our attention and care. We call this kind of single-minded purposefulness כַּוָּנָה, *kavannah*. The Hebrew word comes from a root meaning "direction," and so we understand kavannah to mean "with a single direction."

Mitzvah and kavannah

As we perform each task in our life with kavannah, we see that task as more than just something being done. It becomes a consecrated task, a holy obligation, to us. In this way, the world becomes a place filled with holiness. Every

The prophet Isaiah says of God, "Behold His reward is with Him and His work before Him." If the reward of all Israel is the World to Come, what is the reward of each Jew, right now, for approaching each task with kavannah?

task becomes the work of holiness and peace, and we change our world through our work into a world full of the spirit of the All-Present, the spirit of the Lord.

Reflection For the world and for the Jewish people, each of us is a new beginning. None of us is required to finish the work of making the world perfect, but all of us are a part of the work. Each of us plays a small part in bringing the work to completion.

We lose our freedom when we fool ourselves into believing that the work is too great to be undertaken. No matter how great or how small a person's part of the work, that remains his or her task, and that person remains the only one who can bring it off, the only one who can make that singular contribution. It was for this purpose we were all created.

Every task that we take on must therefore be performed without thought of immediate reward.

The story is told of a Hassidic rebbe who went to the circus and saw there a man walking a tightrope. When one of his students asked, "Why is that man risking his life in this way?" the rebbe answered, "I do not know why. But I know this, as long as that man is walking along that tightrope, he is using his whole mind and soul to concentrate on walking along it. If for one moment he stopped to worry about the money that he is earning by walking the tightrope, he would be lost and would fall to his death. Only when he concentrates on the task at hand, the work that he has to do in walking the thin cord, can he hope to succeed."

We are all like the tightrope walker. If we stop to worry about the reward of doing this task as opposed to the reward for doing another, we will fail totally to accomplish any task. Instead, each of us must work with kavannah, directing his or her entire mind and soul to the work that he or she alone can do. We may never succeed in completing it, yet we are not free simply not to do it.

Just as no one else can share your sense of satisfaction for having done a good thing, so no one else can perform your task for you—the task is yours alone to choose and it is yours alone to do.

Night had fallen and the Havdalah had been recited to separate the Sabbath from the days of the week. The rabbi sat beneath a tree, lighting his pipe with huge puffs of grey smoke that rose toward the clear, dark heavens.

Two students, seeing that the rabbi was in such a peaceful mood, came and sat by his side. For a while the three sat in silence. Finally, one student spoke, "Tell us, dear rabbi, how should we serve God?"

"Can I know?" the rabbi replied. Then the three fell silent once more, except for the small sound that the rabbi made as he drew upon his pipe in smoking. At last the rabbi spoke:

Two friends once climbed a mountain together and found themselves faced with a deep chasm to cross. Together they managed to heave an anchor across the chasm with a rope attached to it. Thus they created a narrow rope bridge from one side to the other. The first then walked across the chasm, risking his life at every step; but reaching the far side in safety.

The other, still standing in the same spot, cried out to him: "Tell me, dear friend, how did you manage?"

"I do not know for sure," the first friend replied, "but whenever I felt myself toppling over to one side, I leaned toward the other."

22

Seeking the right course

If you lived alone in some island-world, separated from the rest of humanity, the words "good" and "bad" would only mean "what is good for me" and "what is bad for me." Instead, you live in society with others, and you are part of a tradition that gives other meanings to the words "good" and "bad."

Life is complicated, and rules sometimes seem to be made just to be broken. As each new situation appears, you are forced to make choices about what kind of action you will take. Having rules and preferences helps you decide. And people around you are willing to help by giving you advice based on their experience. But in the end the choice belongs to you alone.

Along the road one day came an old grandfather and a young boy leading a donkey by the reins. The trio painted a colorful picture as they moved along, the donkey's head bobbing up and down in time to their steps. All was well until they met a stranger along the road. "Hello there," he said to them. "Why do you walk and not ride? Donkeys are made for riding."

The two agreed that this was good advice and climbed up on the donkey's back.

But as they came closer to the town, people along the road began to

229

gossip with one another. Soon one fellow stopped them. "Such a small donkey," he said, shaking his head from side to side. "The two of you are too great a burden upon its back. Are you not ashamed? It's cruelty to treat an animal in such a way."

Immediately the grandfather and the boy saw the wisdom in the man's words, and the boy slipped off the donkey's back to walk along beside.

They had not gone very far in this fashion when they were met by a peddler pushing his cart before him. "Why do you force that boy to walk while you ride?" the peddler asked the old man. "Don't you think that you weigh too much for that poor donkey's back? Why tire the boy and the donkey when you could walk?"

The young boy looked at his grandfather. They shrugged their shoulders as if to say, What's to be done? For they saw the sense in the peddler's words. It was true that the old man was a heavy burden, though not as heavy as the both of them. Still, the old man could walk and the boy could ride. So the old man climbed down from the donkey's back and placed his grandson there instead.

In this way they proceeded again toward the town. But all too soon they were stopped by the call of a farmer standing by the roadside with his friend.

"You, boy," the farmer cried out, "have you no respect for your elders? It's a disgrace for you to ride and make that poor old man walk."

The farmer turned to his friend and still speaking loud enough for the boy to hear, he said, "Imagine a strong young boy like that making an old man walk while he rides!"

Again the boy climbed down from the donkey's back, for he felt the sting of truth in the farmer's words. But what was to be done now? No matter whom they listened to, someone was not pleased. And all the advice they had got was good advice. It was no good to lead the donkey with no one riding. It was no good for both to ride. It was no good for the old man to ride alone. It was no good for the boy to ride alone. Only one choice was left. With a sigh, the grandfather and his grandson heaved the donkey up on to their backs.

And thus they continued to the town, as the people by the road jeered and laughed to see an old man and a boy struggling beneath the weight of a donkey.

Listening to everyone This may seem an absurd tale. Yet when we listen to everyone around us, we do often end up "carrying the donkey." Everyone by the side of the road gave the old man and his grandson good advice. But each piece of advice was based only upon what that person saw.

Thus the stranger saw a boy and an old man leading a donkey and thought how much better it would be if they were riding.

And thus the farmer saw only the boy riding. He did not know that at first neither had ridden the donkey, then both had ridden, then the grandfather alone had ridden—all before he saw them at all.

The advice that the old man and his grandson received was not really helpful because they never chose for themselves. Yet they were the only ones who could really make an intelligent choice. And the only intelligent choice they could make was to stick with the way *they* liked best. Life is complicated, but how much more complicated it becomes when we refuse to take a stand!

We are constantly making choices, but sometimes we forget that freedom of choice is ours. We can choose to do what we want and what is in accordance with what we believe.

Freedom of choice

הַכֹּל צָפוּי וְהָרְשׁוּת נְתוּנָה.

Akiba said, Everything is foreseen, yet freedom of choice is given.
[*Avot* 3:19]

A sage once asked, "How could we have free choice if God knows all things in advance?" And he answered his own question through this parable:

God is like the keeper of the lighthouse along a rocky shoreline. In the midst of the storm, with the light ablaze in the darkness, God looks out and sees the many ships approaching the shore. From above, He sees which ships will land safely, avoiding the jagged rocks; and He knows too which will smash upon the rocks and be destroyed.

Still, each captain makes his own decisions as to how to steer his own ship and what course to pursue. Some will heed the warning light of the lighthouse; and others will not. Naturally one's chances are better if one sees the warning light and steers according to it. Still, each captain is free to do as he pleases.

Each one must make individual choices and decisions, each one chart an individual course. Wise guidance can always be found in the tradition and the law. We need not let ourselves be confused by the offhand —and often contradictory—opinions of others.

Captain of the ship

Each of us is the captain of his soul. The lighthouse is the collected wisdom of our tradition, the laws that we hold to be God's truth. We are free of these laws—free to obey or disobey them as we please.

Yet, as with the lighthouse beam, our chances are better when we follow these laws. We are free to choose, and the choices are spread before us, but there are also guidelines by which to choose: the values and folk customs of our Jewish tradition.

Just as a captain develops a sense of the sea, a feeling for "what is in the air" and an instinct for the proper action, we too must develop an inner sense or awareness that will guide us when we are unsure. This sense we have called religious awareness. It is our religious awareness that serves us as a kind of rudder by which we steer through the sea of life.

Our two impulses

The power of our ship is in our balance between two worlds. We are created as human beings in a state of animal existence, with all the usual animal tendencies within us. Like animals, we kill in order to eat, hunting when we want. Like animals, we have a desire for power, and when we are young we express it even in our games—playing at being "king of the mountain" with all the seriousness that nations play at being the most powerful in the world. Like animals, we have sexual desires that sometimes threaten to overpower us. Most unfortunately, like few other animals, we hunt our own kind for revenge and for personal gain. Our desire to get ahead, our desire to be somebody important—these are contained in our selfish drive, in what the rabbis called the Yetzer HaRa.

But we are other than that, too. Within us is the desire to please others, to bring a smile to the lips of our companions. We have the power of belief and the power to reason and to doubt. And we have the power to sense what is beyond knowing. As Rabbi Akiba used to say:

Beloved is man, for he was created in the image of God; but it was by a special love that it was made known to him that he was created in the image of God; as it is said, For in the image of God made He man. Beloved are Israel, for they were called the Children of the All-Present; but it was by a special love that it was made known to them that they were called Children of the All-Present; as it is said, You are children to the Lord your God. Beloved are Israel, for to them was given the [Torah]; but it was by a special love that it was made known to them that the [Torah] was theirs, through which the world was created; as it is said, For I give you good doctrine— forsake you not My Law. [Avot 3:18]

MAN THE BELOVED

"In the image and likeness of God"—and so by a special love—were we created. Then, by a special love, we were made to know, through our Yetzer Tov, that God created us.

And what is the special love that makes it possible for us to know that we are created in God's image, that we are the Children of the All-Present, and that the Torah has been granted to us? It is the power of our impulse to do good, the impulse the rabbis called the Yetzer Tov.

An inner balance What makes us human is our inner balance between the Yezter Tov and the Yetzer HaRa. As we have seen before, we cannot live entirely by the Yetzer HaRa. And, what may be more surprising, we cannot live by the Yetzer Tov alone. We can easily see the harm that living only by the Yetzer HaRa might do, but what harm would it do to live only by the Yetzer Tov?

Let's take an example: that of fasting. Fasting helps us remove ourselves from the everyday world, helps us concentrate our spirit on prayer, and allows us to separate ourselves for a short while from our earthly necessity of eating. When we fast, we are acting through our Yetzer Tov to come closer to the spirit of God.

Fasting, then, is good for our spirit. And if fasting one day is good for our spirit, how much better it must be if we fasted two days. And if fasting two days is better for our spirit, we could reason, how much better will it be if we fasted three days, or four, or five—or best, if we fasted until we died?

Or take the rabbi who gave so much to charity that charity collectors would run in the opposite direction when they saw him coming: his Yetzer Tov was being allowed to become so extreme that he was in danger of becoming poor himself and as a result an added burden to the community.

Allowing the Yetzer Tov to rule over us is as bad as allowing the Yetzer HaRa to rule over us. We must rule over them both and seek to achieve a balance within us if we are to be of any use to the community and to ourselves. The Jewish community is in need neither of people acting the part of saints or people acting like devils. It is in need of those willing to lead a balanced Jewish life.

The same balance is needed in our relationship with others. We have been given a formula for achieving that balance in Hillel's famous saying: **Balance in the community**

אִם אֵין אֲנִי לִי מִי לִי. וּכְשֶׁאֲנִי לְעַצְמִי מָה אָנִי. וְאִם לֹא עַכְשָׁו אֵימָתָי:

If I am not for myself, who will be for me? And if I am only for myself, what am I? And if not now, when? [Avot 1:14]

In our relationship with the community we have to seek to balance our personal wants and needs against the wants and needs of others.

In order properly to love our neighbors, we must first love ourselves. A person should try to do things of which he will be proud, so that others will respect him, too.

Rabbi [Yehudah HaNasi] said, Which is the right course that a person should choose for himself? That which is an honor to him who does it and which also brings him honor from mankind. [Avot 2:1]

The right course, according to our tradition, is the middle way in which we come to respect ourselves and at the same time act to cause others to respect us. It is the middle way in which we are happy in ourselves and act so that others will take delight in us, too. In almost all concerns the rabbis divide responsibility equally between our duties toward the community and our duties to ourselves.

For example, Rabbi Yose said:

יְהִי מָמוֹן חֲבֵרְךָ חָבִיב עָלֶיךָ כְּשֶׁלָּךְ.

Let the property of your companion be as dear to you as your own. [Avot 2:17]

And Rabbi Eliezer said:

יְהִי כְבוֹד חֲבֵרְךָ חָבִיב עָלֶיךָ כְּשֶׁלָּךְ.

Let the honor of your companion be as dear to you as your own. [Avot 2:15]

Each of us must keep an inner balance between the Yetzer Tov and the Yetzer HaRa. And in the community we must maintain a balance between duties to self and duties to others. In this way we can each find the way of the good heart.

In both of these sayings we can see the balance between self and community. In each, the author asks every one of us to measure his or her own actions according to his or her "self." And in each the action concerns another person —that person's property or honor. The rabbis realized that since we understand our own wants and needs well enough, we should use our religious awareness to transfer what we understand about ourselves to our actions involving others. This is what Rabbi Eleazar had in mind in his answer to Yohanan ben Zakkai's question concerning "which is the good way to which a person should hold?" Eleazar said: "A good heart."

A feeling for what is right You must develop in yourself a feeling for the right balance. The choices are always your own. No one can choose how to live your life for you, any more than he can receive your rewards for you. You must seek what "a good heart" means to you. If by nature you tend to be too generous, you must learn to balance that tendency. Or if your nature is inclined toward being selfish, you must learn to balance that. Only you can feel the proper balance in your choosing. The best balance always lies within you: "Be not evil in your own sight" [Avot 2:18].

23

Choosing life

רַבָּן שִׁמְעוֹן בֶּן־גַּמְלִיאֵל אוֹמֵר. עַל שְׁלשָׁה דְבָרִים הָעוֹלָם
קַיָּם. עַל הָאֱמֶת. וְעַל הַדִּין. וְעַל הַשָּׁלוֹם.

Rabban Simeon ben Gamaliel said, By three things is the world preserved: by truth, by judgment, and by peace. [Avot 1:18]

You might remember the story of the fish who went in search of the ocean. After looking high and low for it, the fish decided that the ocean simply did not exist. Perhaps you feel that way about what we have studied together this year. What does it all mean when we put it together? Is there a way of remembering what it was all about?

And even so, we have not covered all of Jewish ethics in our study. There is a vast amount of literature on the subject of Jewish ethics, and we have merely scratched the surface. You might say that we have studied only the tip of the iceberg.

Yet we have spoken of some of the most crucial concepts and values of our tradition. We have touched on the importance of the community, the importance of the government, the importance of work, the importance of Torah, and the importance of honor and respect, among other things.

At first, you might say to yourself, "These are the ethics of 'the establishment.' They do not allow me to be free as an individual. They only provide for what is good for the group."

Yet we have spoken of values in our tradition that insure your right to be an individual, that protect you from the misuse of power and authority, and that guard your freedom. These are the values of life itself—of freedom of choice, of sensitivity to one another, of friendship and companionship, of open and honest argument, and of fair and equal judgment.

In these values we can recognize the deepest yearnings of the human spirit. Together, communal and personal values provide us with a basis for a noble human community, a community based on truth, on justice, and on peace.

Preserving the world Of the many groups to which you might belong, the Jewish people is the most demanding. We are commanded: "You shall love the Lord your God with all your soul, with all your heart, and with all your might" [Deut. 6:5]. What further demand could be made?

Yet as we have seen in our study of Pirke Avot, in working out what it means for us to love God, the rabbis have shown that it means following His laws while acting in the human world. Merchants must deal fairly with those who buy from them. Farmers must weigh a bushel by a just weight and not cheat their customers. A person must not withhold wages from his or her employee even overnight —payment of wages must be made on time. Charity is a requirement for all—even the poor should find ways of doing charity. Gemilut Hasadim, acts of lovingkindness that promise no reward, are commanded: we must visit the sick, we must help the orphan and the widow, we must deal justly with strangers, we must assist when the need arises in the burial of the dead. These concrete actions are

LAW AND LOVING

Fairness comes first in Judaism—that is, doing the right things. Next comes deeds of lovingkindness—those extra deeds of Gemilut Hasadim.

the expression on earth of our love for God, these and many more.

But three values in particular are paramount in their importance, and in a sense summarize all the study we have done together. In the words of Rabban Simeon ben Gamaliel:

> *By three things is the world preserved: by truth, by judgment, and by peace. [Avot 1:18]*

When it comes to truth, we must trust one another. We are dependent on one another so much that trust has become the deepest bond in all human relationships. We trust others to teach us our tradition that is our birthright, and we trust that they will give it to us truly so that we might judge it for ourselves. A famous story about Hillel and Shammai was told by the rabbis in order to show how trust is the basis for all learning.

By truth

A nonbeliever came to Shammai and said, "I would like to study with you, but first tell me. Is there more than one Torah?"

Shammai replied, "There are two Torot—the written Torah, and the oral Torah."

Then the nonbeliever said, "Concerning the written Torah which I can read for myself, I will trust your teaching. But concerning the oral Torah, I will not."

So Shammai refused to teach him at all.

The same nonbeliever came to Hillel and asked the question again. He received the same reply.

"Teach me only the written Torah," he said to Hillel. And Hillel agreed.

On the first day of lessons, Hillel taught the nonbeliever the Aleph-Bet. He repeated the letters over and over in the correct order so that the heathen might learn them. "Aleph, Bet, Gimel, Dalet . . ."

But on the second day, when he went to review, Hillel began, "Aleph, Gimel, Dalet, Bet . . ."

"Stop," cried the nonbeliever in confusion. "Yesterday you taught me, 'Aleph, Bet, Gimel, Dalet . . .' and today you teach me, 'Aleph, Gimel, Dalet, Bet . . .' Which is the truth?"

Then Hillel replied, "You must trust me for the truth of the Aleph-Bet. In the same way, you must also trust me for the truth of our Tradition." [Shab. 31a]

In the same way, we must trust one another for the truth of our tradition.

In this book we have studied the sayings of Pirke Avot and have allowed them to stand for the tradition of Jewish knowledge. The world relies upon the Jews to master this tradition and to keep it alive. It is a tradition of truth that

we have passed on from generation to generation, reviewing it and enlarging it.

Now it is your responsibility as a Jew to search for truth. It is a responsibility for which you are chosen, and because of it the Jews are called the Chosen People. Yet the truth is not far from you—it is in your mind and in your heart. You must learn to trust yourself, learn to judge for yourself, and learn to decide for yourself. You are the most recent link in the chain of our tradition, through study and through searching you must learn the truth. The generations to come will rely upon you for their birthright, hoping that you will pass on the tradition that you have learned in all its fullness. You are the truth of what will be.

We have also studied the important part that you play as a judge of yourself and of the world around you. And in his saying, Rabban Simeon reminds us that one of the three pillars on which rests the world of civilization is the pillar of judgment.

By judgment

Notice that Simeon did not use the word "justice"; rather he chose to say "judgment"—meaning judgment as in a court of law. And underlying this slight difference in Simeon's choice of words is a difference in meaning. For, on the one hand, justice is blind, as the saying goes: in the eyes of the law all things are equal and there are no special circumstances.

But judgment is not blind: in the eyes of the judge, every case is a special case and all circumstances differ. We need only recall the story of the hat-passing judge who taught his townspeople the difference between justice and mercy in order to understand what Rabban Simeon had in mind when he used the word "judgment."

We may learn from his choice of wording that justice is not a pillar of the community until we put it into action. We must judge others fairly, not just speak of fair play. We must deal with others honestly, not just talk of honesty. We must treat others with respect, not just speak of our generosity and righteousness.

Many people claim to be sensitive, but only those whose actions are directed toward the needs of others in addition to their own needs are truly sensitive. We must act according to the judgments we make about ourselves and about others—then our judgments will be truthful.

By peace Elsewhere in the Talmud a commentary observes that Rabban Simeon's three values—judgment, truth, and peace—are really one, for truth and justice are necessary for peace to exist and are its surest safeguards.

> When judgments are rendered fairly, then truth is upheld, and the result is peace. [Jerus. T., Taanit 68a]

To the rabbis, peace is the natural state of humanity. It is the only way of life that deserves to be permanent. As we saw earlier in our discussion on the value of peace (Chapter 20), a person cannot wait for peace to find him—he must actively "pursue" peace.

The relationship among peace, judgment, and truth is so

close, Pirke Avot tells us, that violence is the unavoidable result when justice is denied and truth perverted:

חֶרֶב בָּאָה לָעוֹלָם עַל עִנּוּי הַדִּין. וְעַל עִוּוּת הַדִּין. וְעַל הַמּוֹרִים בַּתּוֹרָה שֶׁלֹּא כַהֲלָכָה:

The sword comes into the world for the delay of justice, and for the perversion of justice, and for the sin of interpreting the Torah not according to its true sense. [Avot 5:11]

When we wait and wait and do nothing about righting an unjust situation, we more or less invite violence. When the poor of a country are downtrodden and starved, for example, and when the rich totally ignore the plight of their suffering neighbors, then rebellion and revolution may easily come about. When justice is perverted and courts hand down decisions influenced by bribery or political interests, then too violence is not far offstage. When courts fail to judge people equally and instead judge them according to the color of their skin or their religion or social standing, violence might well result—for if the courts are not fair, where else can people peacefully turn?

Paths of peace

Peace is the true goal of the path of the good heart. It is the vision and the dream of the Jewish people. It is at the heart of Jewish ethics and Jewish values. And it is at the heart, too, of the Jewish way of life. Yet it is only one of the three pillars that, according to Simeon's saying, uphold the world. And that should remind us that peace without justice is not true peace, and that peace without truth cannot endure. As the most recent link in the great chain of our tradition, you must seek not only peace in your world, but truth and justice as well.

This is the real test of your own values, of your ability to trust yourself and your religious awareness and to walk in the path of peace. It is to this point that all our study in Pirke Avot has led us: back to you.

Acting Jewishly is not an easy task. It requires that we keep our goal constantly in sight. When our conflicts in-

THE WORLD PRESERVERS

By truth, by justice, by peace—by these three values is the world preserved. But not one of them comes about by chance. All must be sought after, all pursued.

volve realities like trying to decide whether to go to a Friday night football game or attend Friday evening services at the synagogue or temple, or whether to attend religious school or go on a camping trip with friends, keeping our end goal in sight might seem as difficult as clinging to a wall of ice. But what kind of respect would we have for a football player who constantly forgot which goal line he had to cross to score six points?

Choose well   *In a small town there lived a wise rabbi whose fame had spread far and wide. Jews from miles around would come to the rabbi to get his opinion on this problem or that, or merely to listen as he taught Torah.*

In the same town, there was a young student who was jealous of the rabbi. "I am as smart as that old man," the student thought. "Why are people so impressed with his wisdom?" So the student set himself the task of dreaming up a question that the rabbi could not answer. "Then all the Jews who flock around the rabbi will see that the wise rabbi is just a fake," the student thought.

Time and again the student came to the House of Study where the men gathered around the rabbi to ask and to listen. Each time the student would ask the rabbi what the student thought was a difficult question. But each time, to the great disappointment of the jealous student, the rabbi would answer.

Finally the student thought of a clever plan. He caught a small bird and brought it before the rabbi, holding it between his two hands so that it could not be seen.

"Rabbi," the student said, "I have a question that you cannot answer. Between my hands I am holding a tiny bird. Tell me, Wise One, is the bird living or is it dead?"

CHOOSING LIFE

**We choose life when we choose
the way of truth, of justice, and of
peace. We must choose well, too,
what we do with our lives.**

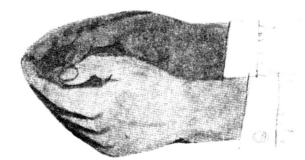

*A strange question! The people present gathered closer together to
await the rabbi's answer. But how would the rabbi know?*

*And the student smiled. For he was sure that the rabbi could not
answer this question. For he had a clever plan indeed. If the rabbi
answered, "The bird is dead," then the boy would open his hands and
the bird would fly away. And if the rabbi answered, "The bird is
alive," the student would quickly crush the tiny bird with his palms,
then open his hand and reveal a dead bird.*

*For a while the rabbi sat deep in thought. His eyes were closed and
his left hand stroked his beard. At last he opened his eyes and looked
directly into the eyes of the student.*

*"My son," he said, "in your hand you are holding a life. Choose
well what you will do with it."*

In every generation we Jews are asked again to renew our
convenant. In every generation we are asked to choose to
continue the long chain of our tradition.

You are being asked right now. You are not being asked
to complete the task, but you are not free to abstain from it,
either. By birth and by heritage, you have been chosen to
continue the task of Judaism, the preservation of truth, of
justice, of mercy, and of peace. In this moment, you are
being addressed by that wise rabbi:

"In your hand you hold your own life. Choose well what
you will do with it."

Right now, you must make your choice through action. If
not now, when?

The Rabbis of Pirke Avot

The early Zuggot

From the time of the Maccabees (approximately 165 B.C.E.) until the beginning of the first century C.E., Palestinian Jewry was led by the *Zuggot*, "pairs" of leaders. One member of each pair usually served as the *Nasi*, or patriarch, whose duty it was to negotiate and direct (as much as possible) the political affairs of the Jewish people in Israel. The second member of the pair usually served as the *Av Bet Din*, and was mainly concerned with the highest court of the Jews in Palestine. There were five sets of Zuggot: (1) Yose ben Yoezer and Yose ben Yohanan, (2) Joshua ben Perahyah and Nittai the Arbelite, (3) Judah ben Tabbai and Simeon ben Shetah, (4) Shemayah and Avtalion, (5) Hillel and Shammai.

To give you some idea of what these men were like, here are biographies of a few who have been mentioned in this text:

Simeon ben Shetah (second century B.C.E.) was, according to legend, the brother of Salome Alexandra, wife of the Jewish emperor Alexander Yannai. If the legend is true, Simeon used this influential position as brother-in-law to the emperor to bring the Pharisee party back into political power in Palestine.

Shemayah (first century B.C.E.) was a pupil of Judah ben Tabbai. His Hebrew name is made up of two words meaning "he heard the Lord." Shemayah and his partner, Avtalion, may have been the teachers of Hillel.

Avtalion (first century B.C.E.) was also a pupil of Judah ben Tabbai. His Hebrew name is derived from two Hebrew words meaning "father of little children."

Hillel (first century B.C.E. to first century C.E.) was Nasi during the reign of King Herod the Great. He founded a school of thought known as Bet Hillel (The "House" of Hillel). The arguments between the factions of Hillel and Shammai became famous, and were continued until the second century C.E. For his good works and fatherly attitude, Hillel became known as Hillel the Elder. Hillel is credited with the authorship of the Golden Rule in its negative form, "Do not unto others what is hateful to yourself."

Shammai (first century B.C.E. to first century C.E.) founded a school of thought known as Bet Shammai which rivaled Bet Hillel in scholarship. Shammai's legal opinions (and those of his followers) were usually very strict. The Talmud records 316 controversies between the two schools of thought. Of these, only 55 times the opinions of Bet Shammai were more lenient. In general, the opinions of Bet Hillel have been preferred in traditional Jewish law.

The Tannaim

From the time of Hillel, the teachers and sages of Israel (whose sayings are recorded in the Mishnah) were usually called *Zekenim*, Elders. But tradition has given them the name *Tannaim*, Teachers. The Tannaim are usually divided into five or six generations, one generation having taught the masters of the next generation. Here are biographies of some Tannaim whose teachings have appeared in this text.

Tannaim from 10 to 80 C.E.

Yohanan ben Zakkai may have been the youngest student of Hillel, though his life is so surrounded by legend that we cannot tell what of his biography is factual. He was said to have lived for 120 years, spending 40 years in business, 40 years studying Torah, and 40 years teaching. Yohanan's greatest achievement was gaining permission from the Romans to found an academy at Yavneh which became the spiritual center of Judaism after Jerusalem and the Temple were destroyed.

Tannaim from 80 to 120 C.E.

Gamaliel II was so greatly admired that he was given the honorary title *Rabban*, which means "our master." He was president of the Great Assembly in Jerusalem. Gamaliel was the grandson of Hillel and taught that Judaism's most central values are peace, friendship, and harmony.

Hanina ben Dosa was a student of Yohanan ben Zakkai. He acquired a reputation as a miracle worker, supposedly performing cures through his prayers for the sick; and told many tales of wonder which were recorded. He was poverty-stricken through his entire lifetime.

Ben Hai Hai is believed to have been a convert to Judaism, and because he studied with Hillel, it may have been Hillel who converted him, just as Hillel had converted so many others.

Yose was a student of Yohanan ben Zakkai and one of Yohanan's favorites. He was called Yose HaCohen (Yose the Priest) because he was descended from the *Cohanim*, the priestly class.

Eliezar ben Hyrcanus began his studies late in life, studying under Yohanan ben Zakkai at the academy in Jerusalem. Eliezer accompanied Yohanan to Yavneh where he became a member of the new Sanhedrin (Assembly). Eliezer established his own academy in Lydda. Once, in a heated debate, he argued against the entire Sanhedrin. When the Sanhedrin decided against him, he removed himself from his colleagues and spent many years in solitude. The Sanhedrin excommunicated Eliezer, but when they heard that he was dying, the Sanhedrin lifted the ban on Eliezer.

Joshua ben Hananiah, a Levite, sang in the choir of the Second Temple until its destruction. He helped Yohanan ben Zakkai to escape Jerusalem and when Yohanan died, Joshua became leader of the Sanhedrin at Yavneh. Joshua was especially known for his defense of Judaism before the Roman emperor Hadrian. Like Simeon ben Shetah, Joshua refused to take money for teaching, earning his small living as a smith or needle-maker.

Eleazar ben Arach was a brilliant mystic. He was one of Yohanan ben Zakkai's finest pupils, and when his teacher died, Eleazar moved to the resort village of Emmaus. In this small village, separated from the other rabbis, scholars, and students, Eleazar's knowledge of Torah rapidly deteriorated. At last, his colleagues and friends were moved to pray for him, whereupon—according to the legend— his great learning was restored.

Eleazar ben Azariah was said to have been a direct descendant of Ezra the Scribe. He studied under Eliezar ben Hyrcanus and served for a brief time as Nasi. Tradition tells us that he was only 17 years of age when he was elected to this position. Eleazar was so wealthy that it was said of him, if a person saw his figure in a dream, that person would soon find great fortune. Still, Eleazar was a humble man and used his great wealth for charity and good works.

Tannaim from 80 to 139 C.E.

Tarphon was a colleague of Rabbi Akiba. He studied and taught with such devotion that he earned the title "Teacher of all Israel." He once said, "Man dies only from idleness, from not working." [ARN 11]

Akiba began his studies in earnest at the age of 40 and was taught by Eliezer ben Hyrcanus and Joshua ben Ḥananiah among others. Akiba arranged the Oral Tradition according to subjects, a text which became a partial basis for the Mishnah. Akiba was the most prominent of the Tannaim. He had thousands of students. During the revolt against Rome, Akiba supported Bar Kochba. He died a martyr, cruelly executed by the Romans.

Tannaim from 120 to 139 C.E.

Ishmael ben Elisha was taken captive as a young boy and held for ransom by the Romans. Joshua ben Ḥananiah ransomed him and instructed him in Torah. Ishmael developed 13 famous principles for interpreting the Torah and laid the groundwork for the *Mechilta*, the *Sifre*, and other midrashic works.

Simeon ben Azzai was a colleague of Akiba and ben Zoma. Simeon was never ordained, yet he ranked with the great masters of his generation. He was known for his great piety and for his lovingkindness. He never married, devoting all his time to study. Simeon taught (as did many other rabbis) that the greatest value of Judaism is respect for our fellow human beings.

Simeon ben Zoma was one of the scholars, like Akiba, to become renowned for his studies in mysticism in addition to his studies of the law. Simeon ben Zoma, like Simeon ben Azzai, was never ordained. Yet he was considered by the rabbis of his generation as an equal in scholarship and wisdom. They said that anyone who saw Simeon ben Zoma in a dream could expect scholarly wisdom to follow.

Eleazar of Bertota was a student of Joshua ben Ḥananiah. Eleazar disagreed with Akiba frequently. He probably spent most of his years in Yavneh and was best known for his charity. He gave so much and so often that he was in danger of impoverishing himself and his family. Hence, the charity collectors tried to avoid him.

Tannaim from 139 to 165 C.E.

Meir studied with Akiba. He earned his living as a scribe. One time he spent Purim in a community which had no *Megillat Esther* (Scroll of Esther) from which to read. Meir wrote the entire scroll from memory! He was so brilliant that the Talmud records that if the discussion of the majority of the rabbis differs from Meir, it is because the other rabbis could not "plumb the depths of his reasoning." He married the daughter of Ḥananiah ben Tradion, a woman named Beruriah who was considered a scholarly authority by the rabbis.

Simeon ben Yoḥai studied with Akiba for 13 years and was personally ordained by Akiba. Because of his anti-Roman teaching, Simeon and his son were forced to hide in a cave near Gedera for 13 years. Afterward, he founded an academy at Miron, dying there, according to tradition, on Lag ba-Omer. For centuries, Jews have memorialized him yearly on the festival of Lag ba-Omer by visiting his tomb. Along with Eleazar ben Yose, Simeon went to Rome in his late years to persuade the Roman emperor to repeal anti-Jewish laws. Remarkably, he was met with success and the laws were repealed. Simeon gained a reputation as a miracle worker and was such a renowned mystic that he was credited with having authored the *Zohar*, the mystical commentary on the Bible.

Eleazar ben Ḥisma was a student of Akiba and Rabban Gamaliel II, but mainly of Joshua ben Ḥananiah. Eleazar was best known for his dual mastery of Torah and the sciences.

Tannaim from 165 to 200 C.E.

Yehudah HaNasi was the son of Simeon ben Gamaliel II. He succeeded his father as Nasi. He spent a great deal of his time completing the editing of the Mishnah, working with earlier versions by Akiba, Meir, and Hillel. Yehudah was so highly regarded in his time that he was called *Rabbenu HaKadosh* (Our Holy Teacher). Also respected for his learning and his remarkable memory, he is referred to by the other rabbis simply as *Rabbi*—a mark of the highest honor. He was very wealthy, using his riches to assist other scholars and further the study of Torah.

Simeon ben Eleazar was a student of Meir. He was considered one of the finest minds of his generation, even though his name appears only seven times in the whole Mishnah.

Eleazar HaKappar Berebi was a student of Yehudah HaNasi. He spent most of his life teaching in Lydda. There he taught Joshua ben Levi who became one of the great scholars of the next generation.

The Amoraim (third to sixth centuries C.E.)

The great work of interpreting the Oral Tradition next passed into the hands of the rabbis of the Talmud who are known as *Amoraim* (Inter-preters), from the Hebrew *amar*, to speak. Since Pirke Avot was a part of the Mishnah, most of the rabbis mentioned in our study were Tannaim. But two very important Amoraim deserve special mention.

Joshua ben Levi (third century C.E.) instituted many of our present-day synagogue practices. During his lifetime, he was the accepted head of the Jewish community in Palestine. His authority in legal matters was widely recognized and he was known far and wide for his keen scholarship. Many legends grew up around him which credit him with knowing the Prophet Elijah and visiting Paradise.

Ashi (ca. 355-428 C.E.) was a Babylonian Amora. For 56 years, Ashi was the head of the great academy at Sura and completed most of the work of arranging and editing the Babylonian Talmud. He taught the Talmud in cycles of two tractates a year, completing it once in 30 years.

A Glossary of Sources

Avot de Rabbi Natan (ARN) is a midrashic expansion of Pirke Avot. It may even have been completed before Pirke Avot was finalized, using an earlier version of the rabbis' sayings than the one we now know.

Arachin (Arach.) is a tractate in the Mishnah and Talmud explaining the rules for redeeming that which is pledged to God. Arachin is a part of the Order called Kodashim (Holy Things).

Baba Batra (Baba B.) is a tractate of the Mishnah and Talmud; the name means "The Last Gate." Baba Batra speaks mainly of the laws of inheritance, of business, and of real estate.

Baba Kamma (Baba K.) is a tractate of the Mishnah and Talmud; its name means "The First Gate." Baba Kamma deals with laws of buying and selling, of loans, and of rental.

Baba Metzia (Baba M.) is a tractate of the Mishnah and Talmud; its name means "The Middle Gate." It speaks of the laws of damages to persons and properties. The three "Gates" are all found in the Order called Nezikin (Damages).

Berachot (Ber.) is the first tractate of the Mishnah and Talmud, a part of the Order called Zeraim (Seeds). Berachot deals with blessings and prayers, and begins with a discussion on the Shema.

Deuteronomy Rabbah (Deut. R.) is a collection of the legends and explanations surrounding the book of Deuteronomy. See *Midrash Rabbah*.

Ecclesiastes Rabbah (Eccles. R.) is a collection of legends and explanations built on the sayings found in the biblical book of Ecclesiastes (Hebrew: *Kohelet*). See *Midrash Rabbah*.

Erubin (Erub.), a tractate of the Mishnah and Talmud, is a part of the Order Moed (Festivals). Erubin is a discussion of the problems of traveling on Shabbat.

Esther Rabbah (Esther R.) is made up of the legends surrounding the story of Queen Esther as found in the Bible. See *Midrash Rabbah*.

Exodus Rabbah (Exod. R.) is a collection of legends and explanations on the book of Exodus. See *Midrash Rabbah*.

Genesis Rabbah (Gen. R.) is made up of legends and explanations surrounding the book of Genesis.

Jerusalem Talmud (Jerus. T.) is the name given to the discussions, commentary, and legal decisions based on the Mishnah; it was compiled by the rabbis (Amoraim) in Palestine toward the end of the fourth century C.E. Much of the original is lost, and even the parts which remain are much shorter than the Talmud compiled in Babylonia which is now called simply *the* Talmud.

Ketubot (Ket.), a tractate of the Mishnah and Talmud, is a part of the Order called Nashim (Women). Ketubot deals with the laws of marriage agreements, and the laws of divorce.

Kiddushin (Kid.), a tractate of the Mishnah and Talmud, deals with betrothal and engagements, and the laws of valid marriages. The word Kiddushin means "Holiness" and is one of the Hebrew names for marriage and the marriage ceremony. This tractate is also a part of Nashim (Women).

Leviticus Rabbah (Lev. R.) is a collection of midrashim and commentary surrounding the book of Leviticus. See *Midrash Rabbah*.

Makkot (Mak.), a tractate of the Mishnah and Talmud, is a part of the Order Nezikin (Damages). Makkot (from the Hebrew word meaning "whippings") discusses those crimes punished in ancient times by whipping.

Mechilta is a name used for certain ancient collections of Midrash. The term Mechilta is Aramaic and means "measure."

Midrash Rabbah is the most important collection of midrashim and is made up of ten collections, each of which is built around a book of the Bible. The word Midrash has the meaning "explanation," and the Midrash Rabbah contains explanations of the Bible, as well as related legends, homilies, and historical information, given by the rabbis over a number of generations.

Mishnah is the name given to a kind of codebook of Jewish law which was completed by Rabbi Yehudah HaNasi (and his son and followers) between the years 160 and 200 C.E. Earlier versions may have been compiled by Hillel, Rabbi Akiba, and Rabbi Meir for use in teaching their students.

The Mishnah is divided into six Orders and the Orders are divided into tractates. One of these tractates is called Avot and consists of five chapters. When Avot was added to the Siddur (the traditional prayerbook), a sixth chapter was added and the work became known as Pirke Avot.

Nedarim (Ned.), a tractate of the Mishnah and Talmud, is a part of the Order called Nashim (Women). Nedarim deals mainly with the laws of vows.

Pesahim (Pes.), a tractate of the Mishnah and Talmud, is found in the Order called Moed (Festivals), and discusses the laws of Passover.

Pesikta Rabbati is a collection of midrashim surrounding the holy days and special Sabbaths which make up the Jewish calendar.

Pirke de Rabbi Eliezer is one of the most interesting of the collections of midrashim. It was probably completed around the eighth century C.E. The first section is built mainly around the story of Creation and continues through the story of Miriam, Moses' sister. The second section consists of legends surrounding a part of the prayerbook.

Sanhedrin (Sanh.), a tractate of the Mishnah and Talmud, is found in the Order called Nezikin (Damages); in the main it discusses the organization of the court system and the administration of justice.

Siddur is the Hebrew name for the traditional prayerbook. The word *siddur* comes from the Hebrew root meaning "order."

Sifra is a collection of midrashim and explanations around the book of Leviticus. The legends and thoughts collected here differ from those collected in Leviticus Rabbah—the emphasis here is legal.

Sifre is a collection of midrashim based on the books of Numbers and Deuteronomy and differing from the Deuteronomy Rabbah collection.

Shabbat (Shab.), a tractate of the Mishnah and Talmud, deals with the laws of Sabbath observance and the Ten Commandments. It is found in the Order Moed (Festivals).

Sukkot (Suk.), a tractate of the Mishnah and Talmud, describes the laws of the harvest festival and the rules for building and using a *sukkah*. It is also included in the Order Moed (Festivals).

Talmud is the name given to the commentary compiled in Babylonia around the end of the fifth century C.E. (The commentary itself is sometimes called *Gemara*, "finishing" or "studying," while the Gemara and Mishnah together are called Talmud.) This Babylonian Talmud is a far greater work than the smaller Jerusalem Talmud, and throughout the ages it has been preserved intact to be constantly studied and commented upon.

Tanhuma Buber (Tanh. B.) is a collection of midrashim (edited by the famous scholar, Solomon Buber, 1827–1906) most interesting for its arrangement. The opening phrase in each part is *"yelamdenu rabbenu"* ("Let our master teach us"). It was built around the Palestinian custom of completing the reading of Torah once every three years.

Tanna de be Eliezer (Tan. d. b. El.) is a Midrash collection, also known as *Seder Eliyahu*, probably completed in the ninth century C.E.

Taanit, a tractate of the Mishnah and Talmud, and a part of the Order called Moed (Festivals), discusses the laws of fasting and fast days.

Tosefta is the name given to a legal text which probably developed alongside the Mishnah. Some of it is lost and some is coming to light only now. The Tosefta is very important to our understanding of the Mishnah and of the Talmud, particularly the Jerusalem Talmud.

Yoma, a tractate of the Mishnah and Talmud, deals with the laws for Yom Kippur. It is a part of the Order Moed (Festivals).

Zohar (Zoh.) is the name given to the most important of all Jewish mystical writings. The Zohar is written like a commentary on the Bible, but much of it is in mysterious language. The Zohar is said to have been written by Simeon ben Yohai, but it is more probable that it was composed centuries later by the Spanish Jewish mystic, Moses de Leon.

Index

Aaron, 208, 210, 212-214
Abravanel, Isaac, 223
Abba Hoshaya, 125
Abraham, 91, 126, 127, 131
Ahavat Hinnam, 218
Aibu, 52
Akiba, 44-45, 48-49, 70, 74-75, 84, 95-97,
    99, 131, 231, 233
Amidah, 51
Amoraim, 37
Analects, 67
Apocrypha, 39
Ashi, 162-163
Avot, 39-41, 200
Avtalion, 73

Babylonian Talmud, 38
Baeck, Leo, 222
Barbuhin, 170
Bar Kochba (Simon bar Koziba), 95
Bar Mitzvah, 57
Bat Mitzvah, 57
Ben Hai Hai, 63
Ben Petura, 48-49
Bill of Rights, 149-150, 154

Cheating, 80-81
Chosen People, 241
Confucius, 67
Conservative Judaism, 195-196
Constitution (U.S.), 149-150

David, 88, 150, 174-175, 177, 206
Decalogue, 69-70
Declaration of Independence, 150-151
Derech eretz, 34
Doyle, Arthur Conan, 225

Einstein, Albert, 126
Eleazar ben Arach, 117, 236
Eleazar ben Azariah, 70, 74, 203, 207, 209
Eleazar HaKappar Berebi, 88
Eleazar Hisma, 84
Eleazar of Bertota, 135

Eleazar, Rabbi, 166
Eliezer ben Hyrcanus, 112-113, 235
Elijah, 104-105
End of Days, 17, 26, 100, 126, 147
Esther, Queen, 221-222
Eved nirtzah, 90-91
Evil tongue, 167

Five Books of Moses, 35, 216
Freud, Sigmund, 97, 222

Gamaliel, 154, 156
Ganzfried, Solomon, 136
Garden of Eden, 26
Gemara, 37
Gemilut Hasadim, 128-133, 220, 238
Great Assembly, 23, 126, 151

Hadrian, 156
Haman, 221
Hanina ben Dosa, 179-180
Havdalah, 228
Hillel, 8, 30-33, 37, 41, 47, 73-74, 83, 107, 114,
    119-121, 125, 133, 147, 160, 196-198, 200,
    211-212, 216, 235, 239-240
Hillel, House of, 196
Hisda, 125
Holiness Code, 106
Holmes, Sherlock, 225
Holocaust, 11, 68, 128
Honi (Onias), 103
Humash, 216

Ibn Ezra, Abraham, 39
Ibn Nagrela, Samuel, 214-216
Isaac, 126, 131
Isaiah, 60-61
Ishmael ben Yohanan, 71
Ishmael ben Yose, 163, 170

Jacob, 131
Jerusalem Talmud, 38
Job, 188-189

Jonah, Rabbi, 73
Jonathan, 174-175, 177
Joshua ben Hananiah, 71, 87, 113-114, 133
Joshua ben Levi, 104-105
Joshua ben Nun, 23, 126
Joshua ben Perahyah, 160
Joshua, Rabbi, 125
Jubilee Year, 90
Judah ben Tabbai, 168
Judgment Day, 53

Kaplan, Mordecai, 91
Kavannah, 225-227
Kitzur Shulhan Aruch, 136
Kodashim, 37
Kook, Rav, 218
Korah, 199-200

Lashon HaRa, 167
Leah, 126

Maimonides, 39
Manasseh, King, 162-163
Megillah, 221-222
Meir, 76-78
Messiah, 97, 104-107, 110, 217
Messiah, Days of the, 19, 26, 99-100
Messiah, Time of the, 101, 110
Midrash, 39, 125
Mishnah, 36-37, 39, 128, 162-163
Mitzvah (mitzvot), 35, 131, 186, 188, 218, 225
Moed, 37
Monobazus, King, 53
Mordecai, 221-222
Moses, 23, 59, 88, 125, 126, 198, 200, 208, 212, 214
Moshe ben Nahman (Nahmanides, Ramban), 39

Nahman, Rav, 190-191
Nahmanides (Rabbi Moshe ben Nahman, Ramban), 39
Nahmias, 154-156
Napaha, Rabbi Isaac, 125
Nashim, 37
Nathan, Prophet, 150
Nathan, Rabbi, 79, 213
Nazirite, 86-88
Nezikin, 37, 39
Nittai the Arbelite, 113

Onias (Honi), 103
Oral Law, 37
Oral Tradition, 23, 37, 196
Orthodox Judaism, 195-196
Oshaya, 158

Palestinian Talmud, 38
Pappa, 125
Passover, 57-58
Path of the good heart, 118, 121, 217, 236, 243
Pharisees, 40
Pirke Avot, 19, 23-24, 30, 33, 39-41, 44, 51-53, 68-69, 79, 83, 101, 111, 127, 163, 173, 199, 200, 213, 238, 240, 243
Prophets, 35
Protest, 103

Rabbis, the, 19
Rachel, 126
Ramban (Rabbi Moshe ben Nahman, Nahmanides), 39
Rashbam (Rabbi Shmuel ben Meir), 39
Rashi of Troyes (Rabbi Shlomo Yitzhaki), 38
Rebecca, 126
Reconstructionist Judaism, 91
Reform Judaism, 195-196
Religious Awareness, 55-63, 64, 75, 94-95, 97, 115, 167-168, 186, 192, 232, 236
Rembrandt, 222-223
Rodef Shalom, 218

Sabbath (Shabbat), 39, 58-59, 73, 93, 228
Samuel, Prophet, 148, 156
Samuel, Rabbi, 166
Sanhedrin, 70
Sarah, 126
Saul, 174-175
Second Continental Congress, 150-151
Seder (sedarim), 37
Seder Nezikin, 39
Sefer Torah, 149
Shalom Bayit, 213, 220
Shammai, 8, 125, 180, 196-198, 200, 239
Shammai, House of, 196
Shemayah, 73
Shmelke, Rabbi, 122
Shmuel ben Meir (Rashbam), 39
Sihon, 214
Simeon ben Azzai, 163
Simeon ben Eleazar, 187-190, 192, 212

Simeon ben Gamaliel, 239, 241-243
Simeon ben Nataniel, 115-117
Simeon ben Shetah, 14-15, 208
Simeon ben Yohai, 135-136, 137, 209-210
Simeon ben Zoma, 70-71, 97, 124, 136, 180
Simon bar Koziba (Bar Kochba), 95
Sinat Hinnam, 218
Slavery, 23, 90-91
Sodom, 134-135, 141-142
Solomon, 130, 206
Spinoza, 222

Talmud, 23, 27, 38-39, 41, 47, 90, 103, 106, 140, 146,
    154, 156, 207, 214, 217, 242
Tanach, 36, 41
Tannaim, 37
Tarphon, 70, 84, 107, 109, 221, 223
Ten Commandments, 67, 69-70, 122, 145
Tohorot, 37
Tolstoi, Leo, 225
Torah (Torot), 23-24, 26, 34-35, 37-38, 40, 44-47, 59,
    73-75, 76-78, 83-85, 87, 89-90, 95-96, 99, 112, 119,
    126, 135-136, 145, 149, 156-158, 166, 196-198,
    203-210, 211-212, 216-218, 225, 233-234, 238, 239,
    243
Tosefta, 39

Urele of Strelisk, 177-178

Vivekananda, 209

World to Come, 26, 59, 225
Writings, 35
Written Tradition, 23

Yavneh, 118
Yehudah HaNasi, 36, 235
Yetzer, 27, 97
Yetzer HaRa (Inclination or impulse to evil), 27, 28,
    29, 31-32, 50, 55-56, 63, 80, 86, 109, 114, 115, 133,
    137, 138, 143, 145-147, 168, 175, 187, 191-192,
    198-200, 233-234
Yetzer Tov (Inclination or impulse to good), 27, 56,
    86, 137, 145-147, 175, 192, 199, 234
Yitzhaki, Rabbi Shlomo (Rashi of Troyes), 38
Yohanan ben Zakkai, 90-91, 97, 111-117, 124-125,
    133, 136, 236
Yose HaCohen, 114-115, 235

Zabara, Joseph, 195
Zadok, 114
Zeraim, 37
Zohar, 24
Zusya of Hanipol, 54, 55-56, 63